COLLECTED SERMONS

Rabbi Yisrael Motzen
Ner Tamid Greenspring Valley Synagogue

CELEBRATING 10 YEARS OF LEADERSHIP AND GROWTH

ISBN: 979-8-35092-235-6

CONTENTS

Introduction -

ASHIRA LASHEM

I use the word 'I' quite often in my sermons.

This is something I noticed as I sifted through my *drashos* from the past decade; as time went on, I spoke about myself more and more. Some may see that as a problem, an expression of the self-centeredness that this generation is plagued by, and at times that may have indeed been a driving force, but I'd like to suggest that there is something that can only be conveyed with an 'I.'

Sometimes the usage of personal anecdotes is simply a hook. In an episode of the Simpson's, Homer becomes a wildly popular college professor because he shares intimate details of his home life with his students. A personal story from the pulpit or shared on social media will get far more attention than a story of Avraham and Sarah. It's a cheap tool, but often benign.

However, some of those anecdotes may serve a higher purpose. The rabbi or teacher may feel like they learned a lesson that can only be conveyed through a personal story. There is value in doing so but there is also great danger. A growing body of research demonstrates how people in leadership positions can lose their humility and empathy over time. The leader begins to see himself as distinct and therefore better than his flock. This is when poor judgment sets in and the scandals that we are all too familiar with arise. Centering stories of religious growth around oneself can too easily lead one down this dark and dangerous path. This is a danger that anyone in any position of power must grapple with and may be a good reason to veer away entirely from using the first-person.

There is, however, a form of first-person preaching that is noble, and in my opinion, needed desperately. In the final chapters of Isaiah, the prophet speaks of a man who has gone through many tribulations. The man speaks of his failures and subsequent disappointment. According to Rav Dovid

Kimche, a 12-13th century scholar, the man in this section is none other than Isaiah himself who is giving us a glimpse of his inner world. Those passages are so compelling that they are known to Christians as the sections of the Suffering Servant (and obviously referring, in

their opinion, to someone other than Isaiah). A far more popular model of first-person literature is Tehilim, arguably the most popular book in Tanach. A large part of its popularity is undoubtedly due to the incredible range of emotions expressed by King David. Throughout the ages, so many have been able to find their own voice expressed through his words. Another example is the most haunting passages of Eicha, which begin with the words, "I am the man." The list goes on.

Many of the people I have looked up to for their ability to convey relevant Torah lessons to modern societies – Rabbi Samson Raphael Hirsch, Rabbi Norman Lamm, and Rabbi Jonathan Sacks to name a few, rarely spoke in the first-person. My early *drashos* were heavily inspired by their style. However, at one point, and I do not remember when, I heard the following quote from Rav Yosef B. Soloveitchik. He was addressing a group of rabbis at an RCA convention and shared with them the following:

"I do not believe that we can afford to be as reluctant, modest, and shy today as we were in the past about describing our relationship with the Almighty. If I want to transmit my experiences, I have to transmit myself, my own heart. How can I merge my soul and personality with the students? It is very difficult. Yet it is exactly what is lacking on the American scene."

Rav Soloveitchik was arguing for what Isaiah and King David did so well, namely, invite their readers and listeners into their inner experience; the jagged edges of their struggles, the awe they felt standing before God, the bubbling gratitude for the blessings received, and their yearnings for an ever-deepening connection to their Father in heaven. It is this type of first-person talk that I attempt to engage in as it invites the listener and reader not to imitate the author – that would be a travesty, but to use the author's inner experiences as a mirror into their own rich spiritual life.

In this respect, a sermon is most akin to a song. There is an introduction that sets the tone and draws in the listener's attention, a verse in which the story, themes, and emotions are laid out, and finally, there is a chorus, a message that the author of the sermon hopes the listener or reader will hold on to. But there is also an especially personal element to a song, often expressed but not limited to its performance, in which the emotions and inner world of the composer comes through. As Tolstoy put it, "Music is the shorthand of emotion." Whether all writing is autobiographical is debatable, but all agree that singing expresses the soul.

A good sermon, in my opinion, is one that conveys a glimpse into the author's inner world. This is valuable not because the author's inner world is richer, but it's an opportunity to provide a vocabulary to guide the listener through the rooms of their own spiritual palace. I have therefore titled this collection of sermons, **Ashira LaShem**, I sing to God, as the *drashos* that I write and deliver are an attempt to convey some of my inner song. The *drashos* in this collection capture themes and emotions that are especially near and dear to my heart – the empathy needed to form a community (Section 1), the wide range of emotions in our relationship with the Divine, from overflowing gratitude to solace in the darkest of time to the frightening fear of not being sure there is a relationship at all (section 2), unique feelings which our ancestors in their pre-State of Israel ghettoes never experiences (section 3), and finally a dream and aspiration that animates every talk and program in our shul.

It is my hope and prayer that the reader can join me in harmony, or even better, be inspired to create their own song, and give voice to the raging spiritual force that lives within each and every one of us.

* * *

I am deeply grateful to the Ner Tamid congregation and community for giving me this unique opportunity to create a permanent home for some of my sermons and for the many messages of support that can be found in the back of this collection. Your financial support for this project and your personal dedication are profoundly appreciated. Though I would like to thank every one of you by name for what you do for our shul community – Ner Tamid is made up of volunteers, without whom our shul would not exist – in the context of this undertaking, I am most especially indebted to our president, Rob Birenbaum, our chair, Pini Zimmerman, and our Sisterhood co-president, Adina Burstyn. Your relentless energy to bring this project to fruition was exemplary. Thank you to my editor, Rabbi Tzvi Sinensky, for your incisive edits and feedback and for dealing with unrealistic deadlines.

Thank you to my dear parents and in-laws, Chazzan Yaakov Motzen and Nechama Motzen, and Rabbi Moshe and Shoshana Shur for their selfless dedication to me and my family, to my many mentors and role models, to my children, Tehila, Shlomo, Shira, Riki, and Miri, for "sharing" my attention with so many others (you are most important!). Lastly, and most importantly, to my life partner and best friend, thank you Hindy, *mahsheli v'shelachem shelah* just barely scratches the surface.

Section I -

WILL WE BE THERE?

IT ISN'T OFTEN YOU CAN SAY THAT SOMEONE HAS TRULY SHAPED YOUR LIFE, much less the lives of your entire family. That is how we feel about you both. Your dedication and commitment to our children is clear. The shul's youth program is excellent and the Rebbetzin's direction over the last year has been both impressive and rewarding. Shepherding our children into adulthood by giving them leadership opportunities within the program is very important to us all.

You have made Ner Tamid a place that we adults look forward to going to every week. The davening, sermons and camaraderie are without compare and the intentionality around relationship building you have instilled in our culture is what makes Ner Tamid so unique in Baltimore.

Thank you for continuing to push us to grow and for being our guides and partners in Jewish life.

I WILL BE THERE

Es chata'ai ani mazkir hayom.

I AM GOING TO SHARE SOMETHING I AM A LITTLE ASHAMED OF. BUT I THINK it's rather instructive, so I will swallow my pride.

It transpired in 2013. I had just started at Ner Tamid. I remember exactly where I was standing when I took the call. It was from a shul member who had recently lost a loved one. They had not asked me to officiate the funeral. I was new to the shul and didn't really know the deceased, so that was fine. But I did not attend the funeral. Not only that: I did not attend the shiva either. I had no shortage of excuses: I didn't have the time, it was a crazy week, and so on. But the truth is that I really didn't know them and I was nervous. What was I going to say to these grieving people? Nothing. I barely knew the person who died. I didn't know the rest of the family at all. So I came up with every excuse not to go.

And now, I found myself on the phone with the family, who were quite upset at me for not coming to the shiva house. And they were 100% right. I should have swallowed my pride, gotten over the fact that I had nothing to say, and just showed up.

I apologized, of course. Profusely. But they ended up leaving the shul.

Rabbi Berel Wein, the famous Jewish historian and longtime congregational rabbi, wrote a book about his experiences as a rabbi. He has a section in which he describes the many times he was enjoying a hard-earned vacation when he got a call that someone had passed away. He often deliberated, torn over whether to return home, until his wife's advice won out every time: "Berel," she said, "people only die once in their lifetimes. This is your only chance to be there for them." (As an aside, after too many cancelled vacations, he decided to only vacation overseas so he wouldn't be forced to make these difficult decisions.)

His wife's wry observation that people only die once is worth reflecting on, not just for rabbis but for all of us. Thank G-d, for the most part we are self-sufficient. Hopefully we are employed. We have some basic level of social support. We're okay. But invariably, there will come times when our basic support systems prove insufficient. We will experience crises when we feel like we're free-falling, lost, living in a deep, deep fog. For most of us, thank G-d, it only happens rarely. But it happens. To all of us. In many cases, other people don't know when we're struggling or in a free fall. But there is one time when it is apparent to all: when we experience a loss. And it's at those moments that we need one another – not just our rabbi, but each other, all of us – to simply be present.

When addressing a mourner, we traditionally say, "*Hamakom yenachem eschem*," "May G-d comfort you." In this greeting, the word we use to refer to G-d, "*Hamakom*," literally means "the place." There are many explanations as to why we refer to G-d in this unusual way. I'd like to share a homiletic interpretation that accounts for this anomaly: the word *Hamakom* may not refer to G-d but to the place surrounding the mourner. If the space, the place in which the mourner sits, is filled with people, that provides *nechama* or comfort. They need not say anything; they merely need to be present. But if the space is empty – if there are no calls, texts, or gestures, and instead the mourner is left to free fall and navigate the fog alone – then there is no *nechama*.

The wisdom of the laws of *shiva* is well documented. Burying a loved one as soon as possible offers the mourner a path to closure. Taking a break for seven days provides the emotional space necessary to focus on the loss. And *shiva* calls provide the mourner with comfort and strength from the community.

To fulfill the mitzvah of *nichum avelim*, comforting the mourner, one need not say anything at all. All you need to do is show up. In fact, the *halacha* is that the visitor should say nothing until the mourner speaks first. And if the mourner doesn't speak, you don't speak either. That's okay. You're there for another person. That's what's important.

We're not very good with silence, so we tend to talk about silly things instead. Or far worse, we're afraid, as I was, that we have nothing to say or that they don't know us. So we protect our pride and allow our fellow community member to sit all alone, in an empty place.

In the very first message that G-d instructs Moshe to convey to the Jewish people, He does not say to tell them that He will save them or assist them. Instead He says, "*Ko tomar livnei Yisrael, eheyeh shelachani aleichem*," "Say to the Jewish people, 'I will be' sent me to you" (Shemos 3:14).

G-d describes Himself with a new name that we don't find elsewhere: "I will be." What does "I will be" mean? Rashi (ad loc.) explains, "I will be with them in their pain." *Imecha anochi betzara*. The very first message that G-d conveys to His enslaved people is not one of redemption or even one of hope. It is simply a message of presence. I will be with you in the future, and I am here with you now.

The same is true for us. G-d was present for us when we experienced slavery in Egypt, we too must be there for others when they experience a loss. *Imecha anochi betzara*. I am here with you, I may have nothing to say, I may not even know you that well. But I am here for you with my presence.

I often speak to people who are going through hard times. More often than not, I don't have any solutions and cannot find words of *chizuk*, encouragement, that will resonate. I know they will fall flat. But over these past years I've come to realize that my job – and not just my job, but the job of every human being, every member of a community – is just to be there. It's not to problem-solve or to fill the silence with noise, but to touch and feel and taste the pain our community member is experiencing to the best of our ability.

That means showing up to *shiva* houses. That means sending someone a one-line text, "Thinking about you," even if we don't know them that well. That means clicking the "care" button on Facebook when someone posts something sad. *Imecha anochi betzara*.

I'll conclude with a poem I wrote a year ago. It was born out of my discomfort with the silence that being there so often entails.

I struggle for words, I bite my tongue, I sigh from the depth of my soul,
Your pain's so deep, my words so weak, am I helping or hurting you more?
My mind can't stop racing, ideas, solutions, I am trying to not waste your time.
My eloquence fails, my wisdom sails, all I muster is one more deep sigh.

To the sleepless parent whose child is lost, to the orphan with nowhere to turn,
To the suffering in silence, calming minds that can't stop, and fears that always return,
To those stuck in bed, with nothing to live for, fighting to go on for one more,
To those haunted by demons, by loved ones who hurt them, who robbed them of all youthful joy.

To those hiding in closets, living two lives, torn into pieces and shreds,
To the voices not heard, the people not seen, they walk among us, the living dead.
To the lonely soul yearning for connection and love, whose hope hardened into despair,
To those who read this and wept, their pain not expressed, truly, my greatest fear.

So as I struggle for words, as I bite my tongue, as you wonder if I'm even still there,

I am trying my best to feel your pain, and to be there with you, and to care.

I don't have solutions, or words of wisdom, I don't mean to waste your time.

I just want you to know that no matter the reason, *imecha ano-chi betzara.*

We may not always have the words. We may be afraid to admit that we don't have the words. But as community members, let's take a page out of G-d's playbook. Let's be there for each other in times of pain.

Sermon Sponsored by
Estee & Robert Fraser and
Helen & Amos Pinchasin

Mazal Tov! Thank you for your leadership and dedication to our families and our congregation! We feel blessed and honored to be in the Ner Tamid family. We thank you for welcoming our family to Baltimore and for your tremendous efforts bringing us and many new members into this incredible community. We have no words to describe the feelings we have when our son describes looking forward to being in shul, attending your classes, and hearing you speak. Thank you for all you do. We wish you a lifetime of health, happiness and hatzlacha! Looking forward to supporting you in service to Ner Tamid!

* * *

In memory of Tamar bat Avraham, Rachel Bayas bat Avraham and Edna bat Chaim, sisters and niece of Amos Pinchasin. Thank you so much for welcoming our family, and Bobby, Estee and Joey to your wonderful shul! We especially loved sharing and participating in your spectacular Seder. We wish you much hatzlacha for many more years to come!

LISTENING FOR THE CRIES

THIS MORNING I'D LIKE TO SHARE WITH YOU THREE STORIES. THE NAMES and details have been changed. You will quickly see why.

Story #1 involves a young boy, whom we'll call Avi. Avi was a bit of a troublemaker. He was always getting himself into conflicts with classmates and teachers. One day he confided to an adult family friend that his father was touching him inappropriately. The family friend informed the school that Avi was attending, but the school, knowing this boy and his penchant for controversy and attention-seeking behavior, dismissed the allegations and did nothing about them. "The boy's a liar." "The boy's a troublemaker." "It doesn't involve us, so we're not getting involved."

This pattern continued for some time. Avi would again confide in this adult, the adult would follow up with the school, and the school would ignore it.

Finally, two years too late, the family friend called the police, who stepped in, arrested Avi's father, and put Avi in the care of a foster family. At this point, Avi had been sexually abused for years, was deeply scarred, and would require intensive therapy to teach him to trust others and not be ashamed of himself.

Someone once asked me if the Torah speaks about child abuse. While it is not mentioned explicitly, I would suggest that it is the mitzvah mentioned the *most* times in the Torah: "Do not oppress a convert, an orphan, or a widow."

Variations of this prohibition are mentioned thirty-six times in the Torah! This week's parsha, which is all about social justice and how to build the fabric of a healthy society, begins and ends with this prohibition. This prohibition is not limited to converts, widows, or converts. It is a principle demanding of us to look out for those who are vulnerable. "G-d hears their cry," the Torah tells us. And we are enjoined to emulate G-d and to listen ever so closely to the voice of the vulnerable and to the pleas of the powerless. There is no one more vulnerable in society than children, who are powerless and completely dependent on adults. So yes, the Torah does speak of child abuse, thirty-six times, and it teaches us to listen to their cries.

I hope this goes without saying, but a story like Avi's should have never ever taken place. When a child, regardless of how big of a "troublemaker" or "liar" he or she may be, shares with us an allegation, we have an obligation – a legal and moral obligation – to pick up the phone and inform the police. We have an obligation to help the child and his family and to care for them. Does an allegation mean something is true? Not necessarily. But if someone cries, especially a child, it's our responsibility to hear their cry and help them. *And let me emphasize: helping and supporting them is not synonymous with passing judgment on the accused.* Not knowing whether the allegation is true does not prevent us from providing necessary support.

Is Child Protective Services perfect? Far from it. Do people get accused of things they did not do? It is extremely rare, particularly in regard to abuse, but it could happen. But I would hate to be the one who made that decision on my own and turned out to be dead wrong. A good society, a righteous society, heeds the cry of the vulnerable, and children are most vulnerable of all.

Story #2 involves a different type of cry. There are audible cries and there are silent cries. This story is about a silent cry. Sarah was a quiet, well-liked, sweet young teen. At one point, in her freshman year of high school, she started to withdraw from her friends and family. Her grades began slipping and her usual put-togetherness was replaced with a complete disregard for hygiene.

Her friends were so caught up in their own lives that they stopped checking in with her and just moved on. Tragically, but also tellingly, she didn't have much of a relationship with her parents, and although they saw many red flags, they didn't really know what to say, so they said nothing. Sarah fell and fell and fell.

Sarah was being abused by a sibling, emotionally and eventually sexually. She was crying, she was sobbing, but they were silent tears that no one bothered to listen for.

As a community and as good citizens, we have an obligation to make ourselves aware of these *silent* cries as much the audible ones. Being attuned to the silent cries means being aware of family members or friends who start acting differently. And it may not be abuse that's going on. But when someone suddenly starts acting very differently, when people start behaving and speaking in ways they never did before, it may be their way of crying out to you: "Help me!"

But it's more. Listening to these silent tears means that you are a *person* to whom your friends and family can turn and share the darkest of secrets, knowing that you won't judge them.

A colleague of mine once commented that he thought there were no issues of abuse in his shul because no one ever spoke to him about it. And then one Shabbos he decided to talk about abuse. He spoke about child abuse, spousal abuse, and elder abuse, all in a compassionate and understanding way. Following that Shabbos, people began approaching him and sharing their stories of abuse. He quickly realized that, of course, abuse exists everywhere. It's a universal problem, and it exists in our community as well. If we want to save people from harm, which we all want to do, we need to transform ourselves into people who are so accepting, so loving that others can share anything with us.

And here I'm going to add something you're not going to like. There's an international organization called Stop It Now. It is a hotline for men with attractions toward deviant behavior. It is set up for people who have not acted on these attractions but are desperately in need of help controlling them.

I don't envy their fundraiser. That's a hard sell. But it's also such a crucial service. The opening section of this week's parsha, Mishpatim, speaks of a thief who, instead of being thrown into jail, is given responsibilities by the Jewish courts in the hope that this will help change the criminal. Judaism believes in rehabilitation, in trying to help even the sinner, and most certainly to help someone *before* they've ever committed a crime.

Are we accepting enough that if, just maybe, a friend of ours had issues that we would justifiably be disgusted by, they would feel comfortable turning to us? Would we be their destination?

Because those people are also crying silently. They are drowning in shame, in self-loathing, and they could be helped. We should listen to their silent cries too, whether that's by checking in when we see warning signs or by being an available and accepting person, letting our friends and family know that we are always there for them, no matter what. Helping them is also helping the victim. These are also silent cries we cannot ignore.

We've spoken about ignoring cries and we've spoken about silent cries, but far more important than these two is preventing those cries in the first place. Our community has made many positive strides in dealing with abuse and abusers. Thank G-d, most schools would not ignore the claims of Avi and would do what they are mandated to do by law. Most schools and institutions would not ignore the signs of Sarah being a victim and would get her help. Recently, many of the local Jewish schools participated in a community-wide program called Safety Kid, under the auspices of CHANA, that educates children about personal safety. If your child's school did not participate, I urge you to speak to them and ask them what education and tools they *are* giving your children. (Full disclosure, my wife is their local coordinator.)

But in addition to the institutional changes, there is a basic change that needs to take place at home. Our children have to be showered with unqualified love and acceptance. Our children have to know that there is nothing they can do that would make them undeserving of our love. Our children have to know that they can turn to us and confide in us. Our children have to know that we are their rock. Because that is one of the best ways to prevent abuse.

Institutions can develop the best practices and policies, which will *limit* the possibility of abuse. But the best prevention starts at home. The safer a child feels, the stronger connection the child has with his or her parents, and the more educated the child is as to what is acceptable and what is not, the safer your child will be.

Which leads me to the third story, a story about Michael. Michael was about as average as a seventh grader could be. He had some friends but not too many. He was a B student, nothing special.

Michael went to sleepaway camp. A counselor at camp befriended him, gave him lots of attention, and they developed a close relationship. One night, the counselor tried to make sexual advances toward Michael. Michael felt very uncomfortable, and he had been taught to trust his intuition. And so he said, "No." And that was it. The counselor backed off.

Then Michael called his parents, whom he knew loved him, accepted him, and would listen to him and believe him. He told them what happened and they called the camp. The camp had protocols, which they followed. They put the counselor on leave and immediately called people in to investigate.

That's my favorite story and that's the storyline we're all shooting for.

G-d calls us a holy people in this week's parsha. As a holy people, it is incumbent upon us to listen when people cry, to not act as judge or jury, but to simply follow the law and call the police. As a holy nation, it's our duty to look out for friends and family, to hear their silent cries, both actively, by being attuned to our surroundings, and passively, by being non-judgmental and accepting. And as a holy nation, it is incumbent upon us, more than anything else, to foster trust, love, and acceptance in our households so that there will be no more cries.

Section II:

BELIEF IN GOD AND BELIEF IN ONESELF

Sermon sponsored by
Pam and David Lehmann

IN HONOR OF RABBI AND REBBETZIN MOTZEN FOR BEING AN INSPIRATION
to the community.

OPEN MY LIPS

The king lay on the floor, not speaking, not eating, not drinking, for days.

In the other room, his newborn kept screaming, inconsolably. The baby's body was burning up. The king's medical staff was useless.

If you looked closely, you could see the king's lips moving. He was praying, or at least trying to pray. This prolific poet, whose every phrase sounded like it was part of a sonnet, was speechless. His words came out garbled. Incoherent. What just days ago seemed effortless now felt impossible.

The king on the floor was none other than King David, poet of Israel and author of Tehillim. The baby was the child he conceived with Batsheva. Though newborns often died in the ancient world, David knew this one was different.

After all, the prophet had just confronted David for having caused the death of Batsheva's husband and for marrying her. Though technically legal, it was a sham, a disgrace, an egregious lapse of moral judgment. The prophet, filled with righteous indignation, sparks shooting from his eyes, unleashed fire and brimstone against David.

"How could you? You, whom G-d transformed from a lowly shepherd to become a mighty king? You, who claimed to be so righteous? You, whom G-d endowed with unparalleled gifts of holy prayer? You?"

When the prophet stormed out and David immediately got word that the newborn child had fallen ill, he knew it was a sign from G-d.

As he lay there on the floor, his entire sense of self melted away. Everything he knew, everything he thought he knew about himself was gone.

I am a humble king! *No, I am an arrogant despot.*

I am benevolent! *No, I am cruel.*

I am righteous! *No, I am a sinner.*

I am a poet! *No, the spirit of poetry is gone. Forever.*

Most of us have never shared David's experience: a moment when everything we thought we knew about ourselves dissipated and we felt utterly lost. But some of us know exactly what it feels like. Maybe you defined yourselves by your wealth, and suddenly the market crashed or you lost your job. Maybe you defined yourself by a role in your family: mother, father, spouse, or child, and then your loved one died, or you got divorced. Maybe you defined yourself socially by the friends you spend your time with, and one day you woke up and your friends were nowhere to be found. Maybe you defined yourself by good health, and even though you work out every day and maintain a healthy diet, the doctor had some shocking news to share. Any of these scenarios can leave us reeling, wondering who we really are.

This past year, I had an inkling of what this may feel like. As many of you know, I have struggled giving sermons these past few months. I fainted while delivering a sermon six months ago. I declined to speak a couple of times. Just two weeks ago, I fainted in shul again. Today, I'd like to share a little of my inner experience during this time.

Before doing so, I want to make a number of things clear. First, you have all been incredible. Thank you. I appreciate all the comments such as, "How are you doing, rabbi?" Or, "No, really, how are you *doing?*" (wink, wink). I am thankful to all those who have chosen not to check in out of respect for my privacy. You've truly all been so supportive and so patient.

I have to say it's been a little entertaining watching you watch me step up to the pulpit every Shabbos. Everyone's on edge. Will he make it? Will he be okay? The new threshold for a good sermon is me not fainting…

Second, I am healthy, thank G-d. My doctor will tell you I am very healthy. I am still exploring all possible causes for the fainting episodes. Every test result (and I'm still running more of them) is pointing to it being nothing at all. Fainting runs in my family. It's unsettling, but it's not a tremendous deal. It's what followed those initial episodes and caused me to be unable to give sermons in the weeks that followed, and likely played some role in the fainting, which was something new for me. I realized after a while that I was experiencing panic attacks. That's right, panic attacks.

I'd start thinking about giving my sermon and my feet would get heavy, my head would start spinning. It would be hard to breathe, and I would not be able to move. Almost every time I got up to give a sermon or to be chazzan, it was – and honestly, often still is – a battle. A crazy battle that rages in my head. Never in my life have I worked so hard. Never. That's the third item I need to get out of the way. To all of you who doubt the intensity or the 'realness' of mental illness, I am here to tell you to stop doubting. And to those of you who are struggling or think you might be struggling with mental health, which, according to national statistics, should be approximately 25% of the people in this room: please, if you're not already seeking treatment, do yourself and your loved ones a favor and get professional help.

Why am I telling you all this? I wasn't planning on it. It's private. It's not anyone's business. I am not looking for sympathy. On the contrary, I hate all the attention I've been getting, and I feel rather silly talking about myself so extensively this Rosh Hashana morning. But I learned something compelling through this experience that changed me in a subtle but powerful fashion. I think and hope what I learned can change us all for the better.

A major component of my identity revolves around standing right here, talking to you. During these past months and especially when this began, in April and May, my sense of self was badly shaken. I could not stop wondering, like King David: Am I done? Am I no longer able to perform the defining feature of the rabbinate?

In retrospect it may have been a little over-the-top, but at the time, it was real and it was scary. Very scary. Heck, it's still scary. Despite treating these attacks in every way possible, they can still happen at any time. It can happen right now. And wouldn't that be ironic…

WHERE DOES OUR SELF-WORTH COME FROM?

So much of our sense of self comes from our job. Or our degrees. Or the house we live in. Or the people with whom we surround ourselves. And it's more than just our sense of self. These identifying markers shield us from vulnerability. They protect us. This pulpit is my fortress. We all have fortresses:

Our resumé, our car, our home, our vacations, our hobbies, our *mitzvos* – they shield us from being a nobody.

Our families, our friends, our online connections – they protect us from loneliness.

Our accomplishments – they ensure that when this body expires, we will live on.

What are we protecting ourselves from? Why do we build these fortresses?

Most of us are protecting ourselves from ourselves. Nobody wants to be a nobody. And many of us believe that to be worthy of not being nobody we need to attain success, especially measurable and visible success.

Maybe our parents only paid attention to us when we were successful; they only told us how much they loved us when we got an A, a job, or a promotion. Maybe we received this message from society at large, which highlights those who succeed. Maybe it's innate. I don't know. It really doesn't matter where it comes from.

Either way, we believe that only when we succeed, materially or even spiritually, are we worthy. I am only a good person because I have this job, or do this good deed, or am friends with this important person, or live in this house, or give to this charity.

Ask yourself the following question: Why do you think you are worthy? Why do you think you are worthy of respect, of being cared for?

Whatever that answer may be, what happens if and when it's gone?

INTRINSIC VALUE

King David lay on the floor, trying to compose words: words that comforted him in the past, words he knew would comfort millions in the future. But he could not. Words stumbled out, but they were empty, flat, childish. Until finally – and we have record of this in the fifty-first chapter of Tehillim – after being confronted by the prophet, after lying on the floor, after feeling so broken, David finally blurted out:

"*Ad-nai sefasai tiftach… I need you, Lord, to open my lips*" (51:17).

At that moment, King David was forced to realize what I hope none of us will ever be forced to realize: everything he thought he knew about himself, and the way everyone saw him, were all a charade. He was not righteous. He was not humble. He was not a poet. He was at rock bottom. "*Ad-nai sefasai tiftach…* I need you, Lord," literally, "to open my lips."

When David said those words, something incredible happened: G-d listened. "Why would G-d listen to me?" he wondered. "I'm a nobody. Worse, I am a sinner." But that was precisely the point. Though it may sound depressing or scary, it is the furthest thing from these. Despite having nothing, despite coming face to face with his mortality and his weaknesses, G-d listened. G-d conveyed to King David that he was worthy. *Just because.* That's right, *just because.*

I am sure some of you are thinking this sounds rather fluffy. You are not worthy just because. You are only worthy when you accomplish. So tell me, what level of accomplishment is needed to cross that threshold of worthiness? Every morning we begin davening with the words: "*Ma anachnu, ma chayyeinu, ma tzidkoseinu*?" Who are we, what great value does our life possess, what great goodness have we performed that any of us can say: "I made it"? Our accomplishments are not what make us great. The entire thrust of Judaism – the notion of our having been created in the image of G-d, the mystical idea that we possess a soul that is a piece of G-d – point to one thing: our accomplishments are nice and important. But our value is intrinsic. We are worthy. We are valuable. We are precious. *Just because.*

BROKENNESS PROPELS US FURTHER

It didn't stop there for David, and it doesn't stop there for us. Once King David acknowledged his powerlessness, a new identity started to emerge. As he began to regain his poetic strength and G-d started to open his mouth again, King David continued just two verses later: "*Zivchei Elokim ruach nishbara*," "The most divine offering is a broken spirit" (51:19). This was King David's new identity: a broken spirit. He no longer defined himself by his actions or his greatness. He defined himself now by what was still broken.

What is a broken spirit? It is *not* the trendy self-help philosophy that proclaims that what is broken is beautiful and calls on us to embrace our flaws. That's ludicrous. It's called broken for a reason. If we accept our flaws, we will never grow.

Brokenness is the opposite of feeling complete. It sounds something like this:

Imagine if we were to wake up every day and ask ourselves if we are being the absolute best version of ourselves. I might ask: "Am I treating my family as well as I can? No, because I am not complete. What can I do to get there?"

Imagine if we were to ask ourselves every time we open a *Siddur* or light Shabbos candles, or sit down to a Yom Tov meal: "Am I fulfilling my duty of carrying my faith? No, because I am not complete. What can I do to improve?"

Imagine every time we had a conversation, we reminded ourselves how much we have to learn. So instead of telling them how great we are and dropping humblebrags left and right, we ask questions, listen, learn, and grow.

Imagine if every time we have an argument, we remind ourselves how imperfect we are, and, instead of accusing, we ask ourselves what *we* did wrong. After all, we are incomplete.

It's a posture, a mindset, a way of life. It is honest and utterly gratifying, even exhilarating.

The moment we let our guards down, the moment we realize that we are worthy *just because*, life begins.

King David's life did not change for the better. In the years that followed, he faced near-impossible challenges: declining health, rebellious ministers, and a son that tried to kill him, to name just a few. His new mindset did not cause his life to have a happy, riding-off-into-the-sunset ending. But it did allow him to find meaning in the darkest of places. It did allow him to never stop yearning for more. And it did allow him to write some of the most evocative chapters of prayer known to mankind. All because of a profound paradigm shift that changed his life: "*Zivchei Elokim ruach nishbara*," "The most divine offering is a broken spirit." G-d loves us, not despite our shortcomings, but specifically when we acknowledge them. And if G-d loves us for our shortcomings, then maybe, just maybe, we can start to love ourselves. To stop hiding, to stop running, to accept that we are worthy. *Just because.*

* * *

My bout with panic attacks is not over. It's a daily struggle. I am still working on it with every tool available to mankind. I'll be okay. One thing I do, possibly the most important thing I do, before I get up to speak, is I whisper those words: *Ad-nai, sefasai tiftach, ufi yaggid tehillasecha.* G-d, please open my lips. I may be a decent speaker who can deliver a nice speech or two, but it doesn't come from me alone. I need G-d to help me. More than that, these words remind me that if I do faint, if I do fail, it's okay. It doesn't really matter, does it? It's not who I am. I strive and hope we can be people who define ourselves by what we do not yet have and what we yearn for.

In a moment we will listen to the shofar blast. *Shevarim*, the staccato sound, comes from the word *shever*, brokenness. Rav Nachman of Breslov explains that *shevarim* represents a *lev nishbar*, a broken heart. This is what I will be thinking about as I listen to that broken sound. I invite you to join me in these thoughts:

G-d, allow me to acknowledge how much I need You.

G-d, allow me to acknowledge how much I need my family and close friends.

G-d, allow me to acknowledge how much I have to learn from each person in this room.

G-d, allow me to acknowledge how much I still need to accomplish, to learn, to grow. Please don't let me ever become complacent.

Master of the Universe, allow me to not feel the need to hide behind my accomplishments. Allow me always to feel my broken heart. Allow me, no matter what I do or do not do, to always feel Your love.

Thank you, all of you, for helping me, for helping each other. Thank You, G-d, for getting all of us to this moment.

Ad-nai sefasai tiftach ufi yaggid tehillasecha.

Sermon sponsored by
The Maine Family

THANK YOU TO RABBI AND REBBETZIN MOTZEN FOR EVERYTHING YOU HAVE done for our family, Ner Tamid and the greater Baltimore community.

JUDAISM WITHOUT G-D

SHABBOS SHUVA IS A TIME TO REFLECT UPON OUR PERSONAL LIVES, TO FIND elements of our personality or lifestyle that are worth changing, and mapping out a plan to do exactly that. Today, I'd like to discuss a trend that affects us both as individuals and as a nation. And it's a trend that is certainly worth changing.

Usually when we think of trends we think of fashion styles; we think of the old pictures hanging up in all of our homes which we look at and laugh. Maybe we think of food trends; I'm sure you all remember the first time someone tried talking you into eating raw fish. And now we have a packed shul when we say the word sushi. Or perhaps the thought that pops into your mind relates to economic trends – how credit cards are no longer a representation of money that we have in the bank but they are now seen by most people as an easy way to borrow money.

Google recently developed a tool called an Ngram viewer that helps measure literary trends. They uploaded millions of books into an online database. All you need to do is type a word. With a click of a button, the Ngram tells you how often that word was used in books in any given year. And they graph for you changes in usage over time. So, for example, if you input a word like "justice," you can see how from the year 1800 and on, the word has been used less and less frequently in American literature. Similarly, if you type "freedom," you can see that over that same time frame, the word has appeared more and more often.

Being a rabbi, I decided to use this tool to observe religious trends in literature over the years. As you probably guessed, the word G-d, from 1700 and on, has appeared less and less in English books. The trend, it seems, is to not talk about G-d. In an opinion piece in the New York Times, Eric Weiner writes: "In my secular, urban and urbane world, G-d is rarely spoken of, except in mocking, derisive tones. It is acceptable to cite the latest academic study on, say, happiness or, even better, whip out a brain scan, but G-d? He is for suckers, and Republicans."

Now you may be thinking to yourself that a drop in the usage of G-d's name doesn't seem to be a very relevant topic for a group of people who were probably here for three hours today praying to G-d and are now back again to listen to a lecture by a rabbi who claims to be speaking the word of G-d. But no, I did not take the wrong notes to shul today. These are my notes for Ner Tamid, not for the atheist's convention, and I do think that one of the most pressing challenges of our time is the omission of the G-word.

And the truth is, I'm in good company. I'm not the only one who thought that deeply religious people struggle with the G-word. The story is told of Rabbi Levi Yitzhak of Berditchev, who once summoned all the Jews to assemble in the town square the next day at noon because he had an announcement of the greatest importance to make. He ordered that the merchants were to close their shops, that all the nursing mothers were to bring their infants, and that everyone, without exception, was to be there to hear the announcement. The people wondered what the announcement could be. Was a pogrom imminent or a new tax? Was the Rabbi going to leave? Or was he perhaps seriously ill? Did he plan to reveal when the Messiah would come? At noon the entire community was present with no exceptions. Everyone waited with baited breath to hear what the Rabbi would announce. Precisely at twelve the Rabbi rose and said: "I, Levi Yitzhak, son of Sarah, have gathered you here today in order to tell you that there is a G-d in the world!"

And today I'd like to tell you the same thing. We need to know, or perhaps, we need to become more aware of the fact that G-d exists. We need to become more comfortable talking about and talking to G, dash, D. And we're not.

How often do we relate a story that has G-d as part of the plot? I imagine not very often. How often a day do we talk to G-d? I'm not talking about praying in the classical sense. How often do we have a conversation with

G-d? I imagine not very often at all. So today, I'd like to discuss: a) why this is a problem, b) why it's a really big problem, and c) what we can do about it.

The problem begins as a small and seemingly insignificant one. You know, all of us are aware of stories that go something like this: "I was terribly sick, I was about to die, when suddenly I rethought everything I knew, I turned to G-d, and lo and behold I was totally healed." Or, "I was in a crazy accident, I blacked out, the doctors thought it was the end, and miraculously I came back." Or, "I was living the life, I had everything I could possibly need, but I felt terrible inside. I met a man who taught me about meaning, etc." Thousands of stories can fit into that template. And all these stories have two common denominators. One is that the main character in the story sees G-d in his or her life. And two, all these stories are dramatic. And who doesn't love some drama? We Americans want *everything* to be dramatic. We've taken cooking and made dramatic televisions shows like Iron Chef – out of cooking! There's a family business somewhere out in Louisiana that sells little contraptions that make a duck call – they've made a television show about them! We don't want information; we want *dramatic* information. Have you been on the weather channel's website recently? They used to just report the news. Now they have videos of crazy people videoing a tornado from a few hundred yards away. They have videos of people escaping a tsunami. In the corner, if you look closely, you can actually find the weather!

So it's no surprise that we want a dramatic G-d. We want a G-d who saves us from illness, we want a G-d who saves us from accidents, and we want a G-d who flips our life on its head.

We want the G-d about Whom we sing every Shabbos morning. You know, if Ner Tamid would have a theme song, I think it would be safe to say that it would be *Mizmor Ledovid*. And in *Mizmor Ledovid* we say, "*Kol Hashem bakoach, kol Hashem behadar, kol Hashem shover arazim*," "The voice of G-d is in power, the voice of G-d is in majesty! The voice of G-d breaks the cedars!" (Tehillim 29:4). In *Mizmor Ledovid* we describe a G-d of drama, a G-d of upheavals and great events.

But there's another section in Tanach where G-d and His voice appear in a very different way. Eliyahu Hanavi, the great prophet, is most famous for his dramatic confrontation with the prophets of Ba'al, a popular form of idolatry in his day. At that showdown, Eliyahu brings a fire down from heaven and proves to the people that "*Hashem hu haElokim*," that there is only one G-d. And the entire nation proclaims right there and then, "*Hashem, hu haElokim, Hashem, hu haElokim*" (Melachim I 18:39)!

However, not too long later, standing at Chorev, G-d shows Eliyahu a whirlwind, an earthquake, and a fire, but G-d is not found in any of these. Then He appears to Eliyahu in a "*still, small voice*" (Melachim I 19:12). He asks Eliyahu twice, "What are you doing here?" (19:9, 13), and Elijah replies both times: "I have been very zealous for the L-rd G-d A-mighty" (19:10, 14).

Rabbi Jonathan Sacks explains that Eliyahu, by responding "I have been zealous for the L-rd G-d A-mighty, was demonstrating that he didn't understand G-d's message. G-d had been trying to teach Eliyahu by not appearing in the whirlwind, earthquake, or fire, that G-d is not to be found in violent confrontation, drama, and spectacle. Instead, G-d is found in gentleness and the softly-spoken word. Eliyahu lived a life of confrontation. G-d was telling him that true G-dliness is found far from the drama. It's at that point that G-d tells Eliyahu to appoint a successor.

Because, you see, G-d isn't always dramatic. Life isn't always dramatic. And the great challenge is finding G-d in the boring humdrum of everyday existence.

I am sure that many of you asked G-d on Rosh Hashana to grant health to you or to someone you know and love. And I'm sure that many of you asked G-d for financial help for yourself or for a loved one who is struggling. There are others here who were asking for peace at home between spouses or children. And that's what prayer is there for – for us to turn to G-d and ask Him for help. But we can't allow the dramatic events in our life to eclipse our need for His help in our everyday living. We forget so easily that our every breath is dependent on His will. We forget so easily that we need Him for everything! We need G-d so that the words that you're hearing right now, coming from my mouth enter your ears! The coordination necessary between my lips, jaw, tongue, and larynx is more sophisticated than the coordination of the most amazing symphony. Those movements create a sound, or more accurately, they create a vibration which moves the particles in the air, which moves the particles next to it, etc., etc., until it reaches your ear. And then our ear catches those sound waves, directs them to the hearing part of our ear, and translates what is being heard into electric signals which can be understood by the brain. We take these things for granted. But we can't. We need to appreciate the fact that G-d is found in our everyday lives; in our every movement and our every breath.

It's like the famous joke of the guy who is looking for a parking spot on a busy street in Manhattan, driving in circles for ten, fifteen minutes. He has a job interview he can't be late for. So as a last resort he turns to G-d and says, "G-d, please allow me to find a parking spot! Please, I'll start eating kosher!" Nothing doing. "I'll keep Shabbos!" Nothing doing. And finally, "G-d, if you find me a parking spot I'll go to shul *every day*!" And just as he says those words, the car to his right zips out of its spot. The man turns to G-d and says, "Never mind. I found a spot!"

I only recently appreciated the depth of this joke. You see, when the man wanted G-d to find him a spot, he understood that G-d finding Him a spot meant something out of the ordinary taking place. He expected a car to vanish into thin air and make way for his car. He expected a flood to wash away the entire row of cars next to him, so that his car would be left with more than enough room to park. That would be G-d intervening. But for the person next to him to pull out? That's not G-d. That's the person next to him pulling out. Where's the divine intervention in someone moving a car at the right time?

But that's a mistake. Because G-d is found in that silent, thin voice. We need G-d to make it through a regular day just like we need Him when everything goes wrong.

Not appreciating this subtle idea is a major theological issue. The first of the Ten Commandments is "I am your G-d." To misunderstand G-d is to violate the first Commandment and possibly the second, the prohibition against idolatry, as well. The Greeks believed in god, but their conception of god was radically different than ours. They believed in the god of drama; it was a god who put the world into motion, but he remained up there. The first Commandment is not, "I am your G-d." It is, "I am your G-d *who took you out of Egypt*." The significance of those words, "I took you out of Egypt," is as follows. In Egypt, G-d manipulated all of nature through the Ten Plagues. But He actually did much more than that. He also distinguished between the water of a Jew and the blood of an Egyptian. He similarly distinguished between Jewish and Egyptian firstborns. That demonstrated two things: 1) G-d is able to bend the rules of nature at will; and 2) He is very well aware of all the details of creation. He knows who is deserving of reward and who is deserving punishment, and He acts accordingly. "I am G-d who took you out of Egypt" teaches us that G-d knows exactly what's taking place here on earth and that He cares. He pays attention to each and every one of us, and takes care of every detail of our life.

One of the principles of faith is, "I believe with perfect faith that He alone created this world and guides all creatures." This is especially true when it comes to human beings. G-d pays attention to every single one of our needs.

It's hard to imagine such a thing. And because we have a hard time believing such a thing, we get very bashful when it comes to prayer. Does G-d really care? Is He really listening to me? Who am I? Why should He care? I believe that that is one of the greatest impediments to meaningful prayer: our skepticism that G-d actually cares about our needs.

Our Sages, in their brilliant wisdom, tried to help us with this challenge. They did so by formulating blessings. Blessings for every food, so that we appreciate and see G-d in the fruits, vegetables, and starches we eat. They formulated blessings for beautiful smells and for wondrous sights. One of the most beautiful is the blessing for one who uses the bathroom, in which we thank G-d for the fact that our organs work so we can properly dispose of our bodily waste. If you've never taken a moment to read the text of that blessing, I strongly recommend that you do so. It's in the front of every Siddur. It is truly a magnificent prayer, which can truly help us become more aware of G-d's never-ending existence and assistance in our daily lives.

Reciting blessings makes us more G-d-conscious and more appreciative. If you say blessings already, reciting them with more concentration will serve the same purpose. And that's my first point: we need to recognize that G-d is in our lives on a day-to-day, moment-to-moment basis. Not being aware of G-d's participation in our lives is a big problem. On the flip side, becoming more aware of G-d will only serve to enhance our lives and our relationship with G-d.

But all this is regular Shabbos morning *derasha* stuff. Today is *Shabbos Shuva*. It's a day to focus on major issues that plague us as a community and as a people. I think the omission of G-d from our personal consciousness has much wider and more dangerous ramifications.

People often ask me, why is it that the Torah, and specifically G-d, is so obsessed with idolatry, *avoda zara*? It is by far the most recurring commandment in the Torah. Moshe warns the Jewish people, "Do not succumb to idol worship," over and over again. Maybe idolatry was relevant two thousand years ago. But nowadays? Give me a break.

The truth is that idolatry was much more sophisticated than we think. I'll use probably the most bizarre form of idolatry to illustrate this point. There was a form of idolatry that was called Ba'al Pe'or. There are a number of strange aspects of Ba'al Pe'or. One is its form of worship: its worshippers would perform disgusting acts in front of the idol. The more disgusting the act, the more praiseworthy was the form of worship. The classic form of service was defecating in front of the idol. The Talmud relates that a certain individual defecated in front of the idol and then used the idol to clean himself. The prophets of Pe'or who were standing nearby commented that no one had ever worshipped this idol in such a magnificent way.

What is the nature of this idol? Idolatry in general is hard enough to understand. But this form of worship is nothing less than bizarre! Rav Chaim Shmuelevitz explains that the very essence of Baal Pe'or was the desire to not be subjugated to any being or power. As a consequence of this freedom, one is able to break all boundaries and rules that come with subjugation to a higher source. All other worshippers recognized the need to respect and honor the focus of worship, but the worshippers of Baal Pe'or strived to uproot the human impulse of genuine service and replace it with degradation of authority. Accordingly, the more disrespectful the act, the greater the form of "worship"! This is why the depraved individual who used the idol to clean himself was demonstrating the greatest "service" to this philosophy – he was showing that he had absolutely no regard for anything at all.

Pe'or is just one example, but once we get past the absurdity of their actions, we start to see that idolatry in general was actually rather sophisticated. Perhaps we no longer feel the same drive as they experienced to serve idols, but it was not an empty and meaningless act. Idolatry was a sophisticated system of worship.

But let's take a step back. Where does idolatry stem from? Or, more accurately, how in a world that G-d created can idolatry sprout up? How did it begin? The Torah indicates that there were forms of idolatry already in the third generation from creation. Imagine that: Adam's grandchildren were serving idols! Let's appreciate the absurdity of such a thing.

Recently, I was putting my children to sleep and I was telling them how G-d created Adam and Eve. They just couldn't wrap their heads around the idea that they had no parents. So let's imagine a dialogue between Adam and one of his grandchildren: "Hey Zaide, who were your parents?" Adam would respond, "I didn't have parents. G-d created me." Yet those same grandchildren, who knew better than we do that G-d exists, somehow introduced idolatry into the world. How can such a thing take place?

The Rambam in his famous work on Jewish Law explains that the first stages of idolatry did not deny G-d at all. On the contrary, the introduction of idols was meant to facilitate humankind's service of G-d. The rationale was that since the sun, stars, and moon are agents of G-d, and they are also entities that G-d honored by placing them high in the sky and allowing them to be the source of light to the world, we should honor them in return. By honoring these celestial bodies, they would actually be honoring G-d.

What drove them to do this? The Mei Hashiloach, the Rebbe of Izhbitz, explained that the concept of serving G-d was overwhelming for them. It was too imposing to constantly be aware of G-d Himself. By serving the stars and the moon, the service of G-d would actually be more accessible. They reasoned that since we all see and appreciate the function of the stars and the moon, and because they are an extension of G-d in this world, let's look to them and through them serve G-d.

But, as the Rambam points out, they made a grave mistake. Before long, people forgot that the sun, stars, and moon were meant to facilitate a connection to G-d. They ended up serving the sun, stars, and moon alone. They forgot about G-d.

I bring this up because I think one of the greatest challenges that the Jewish people face is very similar, a form of what the Rambam described as the early stages of idolatry. We have lost sight of Whom we are serving. Instead, we are serving a part of the whole. We may not worship the constellations, but we are worshipping important ideas that are part of Judaism but not its essence.

Over the years, we have developed many strands of Judaism, what some like to call hyphenated Judaism. Even within Orthodoxy, there are countless "fill-in-the-blank" hyphenated Orthodox groups going around. Not too long ago, *The Jewish Times* had an article about the many boxes and categories of Orthodox Jews. I used to think that the greatest tragedy of all these boxes and hyphens was the disunity it caused. It's bad enough that Jews are a minority and have a hard time getting along with others. But do we really need to distinguish ourselves from other Jews? Especially Jews who all follow the same code of law?

But over time I've come to realize that the greatest tragedy of all the sub-categories of Orthodoxy is not the disunity. Rather, it's that in defining one's niche, when each group along the spectrum finds its cause, whether it's Israel, Russian Jewry, Mashiach, stemming the tide of intermarriage, women's rights, or even Torah study, there is a serious risk of losing sight of the big picture.

All the callings I just mentioned are incredibly valuable. Many groups have adopted one of these callings as their hallmark. Sometimes this is done to draw more people to a more committed Judaism: focusing on a single feature is meant to facilitate greater devotion to an observant lifestyle. Sometimes it's done because the people leading those movements believe that it is the most important thing to focus one's energy on. Either way, I believe it poses a serious risk.

I'll share with you one slightly controversial example. Full disclosure: we recently made a *siyyum* on *Sefer Hatanya*, a book written by the first Lubavitcher Rebbe, a landmark book with brilliant insights. I am also a huge fan of the past Lubavitcher Rebbe, Rabbi Menachem Mendel Schneerson, a man whose wisdom and foresight touched the souls of countless Jews around the globe. But as you know, one of the defining features of the Lubavitch movement was and is their emphasis on the Messiah, on Mashiach. It seems that the Rebbe felt that if people had a tangible goal toward which their *mitzvos* would be directed, they would be more excited to perform them. In other words, you and I fulfill *mitzvos*. Why? Some of us keep the *mitzvos* just because, some because it gives us a more meaningful life, and some because we're concerned about the afterlife. But while some of these approaches may be meaningful, they aren't so exciting. Chabad's message was that if we do *mitzvos*, we can change the world. We can stop all the suffering that we see, usher in peace, and bring about real, stable change. This idea is not exclusive to Chabad. It's found in the Talmud. But what they did is emphasize this point, presumably to give their followers an extra drive and urgency in fulfilling the Torah.

And it worked incredibly well. There is no group in Orthodox Judaism that is as passionate as they are. They will go to the far corners of the earth to help people do *mitzvos* because that brings Mashiach closer. They will have their young children stop people on street corners, asking them, even begging them, to wear *tefillin* in order to bring Mashiach closer. I was personally touched by their enthusiasm. I don't know how but when I was growing up, their children's periodical, a magazine called *Tzivos Hashem*, was delivered to my house. I remember being inspired to do more *mitzvos*. I too wanted to bring Mashiach closer! It works really well.

But it's also incredibly dangerous.

Over time, and specifically with the passing of the last Rebbe, Rabbi Schneerson, a faction of the group veered off the beaten path. You see, the members of Chabad were driven by a messianic ferver. In addition to that passion for Mashiach, many if not all the followers of Chabad felt that their rabbi, Rabbi Schneerson, was the Messiah. When he passed away it was devastating; people didn't know what to do with themselves. They had invested all their energy into seeing their rabbi lead them back into the messianic era – and somehow he had passed away. While many followers of Chabad were mourning, a splinter group arose from the ashes. This group is called the Meshichists; they fervently believe that Rabbi Schneerson is the Messiah and is still alive, albeit in a different form. At their shuls, in the middle of davening, you will hear them proclaim the following words: "*Yechi adoneinu moreinu verabbeinu melech hamashiach le'olam va'ed*," "Long live our master, our teacher, the king, the Messiah for ever and ever." There are even splinter groups from this group which have taken things even further, but I think you get the point. It was a great idea; it was captivating and exciting but it obscured what Judaism is really all about. Judaism is not about fulfilling a particular commandment, it's not about living up to a vague idea of being a light on to the nations, it's not about any specific causes or values; it's about serving G-d. *Anu avadecha ve'atta malkeinu*, we are your servants and You are our king. *Anu banecha ve'ata avinu*, we are your children and You are our

Father. Period. G-d asks us to keep His Torah, to do his *mitzvos*. That is my definition of Judaism. It's not very eloquent but I think it rings true.

I know that when I'm done, and someone asks you what I spoke about, you will tell them I spoke about Chabad. Please don't get distracted by this example. I have an enormous amount of respect for and gratitude to the movement. My point is this: all along the Orthodox spectrum there are groups of people splintering off who represent one cause or another, one mitzvah or another. It's a mistake and it's a dangerous mistake. Whether it's Mashiach, Israel, Torah study, women's rights, *tikkun olam*, whatever. They are all wonderful and important causes. *But let's be children and servants to G-d. Let that be our calling.* We strive to fulfill His will. If we're attracted to one value or mitzvah – that's great. We can have organizations, rallies, and even movements that promote any of these values, but we can't allow them to define our perception of Judaism. We are Jews. We are the children and servants of G-d. No hyphens necessary.

There was a great Torah scholar, Rabbi Pinchas Scheinberg, who passed away not long ago. For some reason – no one really knows why – he wore an incredible amount of *tzitzis*. If you'd see a picture of him, you would think he was a husky football player. But really, it was just layer after layer of *tzitzis*. Why? For some reason, he thought *tzitzis* was a mitzvah that he should focus on, and so he did. But he never started a movement called *Tzitzis*-Orthodoxy! Because he was an *oved Hashem*, a servant of G-d. An expression of his service of G-d was wearing a whole lot of *tzitzis*.

Torah study, the greatest of all *mitzvos*, can become idol worship if a person studies for the sake of the Torah and not for the sake of connecting to G-d. Women's place in religious life, an incredibly important question and cause, can also distract us from G-d for the exact same reason. Israel, the holiest of places, can become idol worship if our religion is no longer about G-d but about a land. And stemming the tide of assimilation, as important as it is, cannot be what defines our religious observance. We can't lose sight of the goal here. It's about G-d. It's about serving Him. We can pick *mitzvos* and causes that we are "into," but they have to be an expression of a holistic, all-encompassing religious life, not one that is slanted and defined by a certain value. It's not that the individual who studies Torah with no thought of G-d is doing so for ulterior reasons. It's just that it's not Judaism. Judaism is serving G-d. Period.

And that is my second point. When we take G-d out of the equation, when He is no longer the focus of our lives, there is a very slippery slope that takes us further and further away from G-d.

So what do we do? How do we bring G-d back into our lives? How do we bring G-d back into the national consciousness?

First of all, we need to start using this G-word a lot more. We need to take G-d out of hiding. People ask, what does the *Halacha* say about this and that? The real question is, what does *G-d* say about this and that! The Shulchan Aruch is G-d's mouthpiece. What does *Judaism* say about abortion? The real question is what does *G-d* say about abortion! Someone here once told me off for saying "the Torah says." He said, "Rabbi, the Torah is a book. If you believe that G-d is the author, then 'G-d says' is much more appropriate!"

And he's absolutely right. I still have a hard time saying it because I wasn't brought up speaking that way – but he's right! If we want to be more G-d-conscious, the place to start is clearly in our discussions of Judaism. We have to remind ourselves that it's all about G-d.

And by the way, it goes a long way. I'll share with you a quick story.

A little while ago, I had one of my most refreshing conversations in a long time. I met up with an old friend. He is a modern-day version of the stereotypical simple Jew of the past. He prays every day, he learns every day, he is a good husband, a good father, and a hard worker who runs a modest but successful business. But there are no games, no airs to him at all. He was describing to me a dilemma he had. He needed a *pesak*, a halachic ruling for a difficult question. Even before asking, he knew that this rabbi would say this and this other rabbi would say that. He knew that either way he turned there was what to rely upon. But as he said to me, "What I really want to know is: *what does G-d want from me?*"

Now of course it's not simple knowing what G-d wants from us. But the point he was making was that he didn't just want the rabbi to rule leniently for him. He didn't just want a ruling that was convenient for his lifestyle. He recognized that G-d stands behind the Jewish legal system. Knowing that gave him a very different attitude towards Judaism than most of us have.

But it's not just in the realm of Jewish law and Torah study that we need to be G-d-aware. It's in our daily lives. There is a wonderful little segment on the Aish HaTorah website called Lori Almost Live. It's a weekly, 2-3-minute video by a woman called Lori Palatnik. She lives in Rockland and helps run an outreach program in DC. She recently started an organization called The Jewish Women's Renaissance Project, a wildly successful trip for women to go to Israel and connect to their Jewish heritage. On one of the videos, she talked about something she does at her Shabbos meal. In order to get dessert at her table, one must share one story illustrating how G-d was watching over them in the past week. Now these stories are not dramatic; they don't involve people recovering from deathly illnesses and being rescued from burning cars. They are stories like bumping into someone that you needed to speak to, having the right amount of change in your pocket, or *finding a parking spot when you really needed one.* These are simple stories where something worked out just the way they needed it to. With her dessert incentive, she forces people to take a moment and recognize that G-d is watching them every week and every day, not just in the dramatic stories we share with people, but in the simple moment-to-moment existence.

There's one last area in which we can bring G-d more into our lives. Until now I've discussed talking *about* G-d, but to truly bring G-d into our lives we have to talk *to* Him as well. I am not talking about coming to shul more often. I am talking about having intimate conversations, in your native language, with your Creator.

I'd like to share something with you. It's very personal and I feel a little uncomfortable sharing something so personal. And it's also simple, and I fear that I will not be able to convey how meaningful this was to me. But share I will.

The story goes back around a decade. I was twenty and I was spending the holiday of Sukkos in Toronto. While I was there, I bumped into some teenage boys. I quickly realized that these boys were not doing well. Broken families, drugs, you name it. So I decided to do something about it. The summertime is the worst time for these teens – they would typically stay home for the summer and whatever they would do during the year, they would do in the extreme over the summer. So I decided I was going to get them out of the city and travel around the United States with them to keep them out of trouble. I started working on this camp, crunching numbers, developing a route, etc. I only had two problems: 1) I had to fundraise $10,000, and 2) I had no campers.

Anyway, it was the day before Purim and I found some people who would fundraise for the camp in New York, but I wasn't sure if the camp was even going to happen. How in the world was I going to talk parents into trusting a twenty-year-old with their children while driving around the country? So I had a dilemma: should I first see if I could find the campers and then start fundraising, or should I fundraise now – people are more generous on Purim – and hopefully pull it all together? And after speaking to some wise people who counseled me to go forward, I decided I would.

But I still wasn't sure if this whole thing was just a pipe dream. Maybe I should just give it up. So that night I took a walk. On that walk I stopped. I turned to G-d and said, "G-d, You obviously don't owe me anything. But I am making a camp and I'm making this camp for You. I don't need it. But these kids, Your children, they need it. Now I have no idea how this is going to work out, but G-d, it has to work out. For the sake of Your children, it has to work out!"

And it did work out. I ran the camp for two summers and the camp eventually blossomed into a sleepaway camp for high school boys in Toronto. But that's not the point. To me, that walk and short conversation with G-d was one of the most spiritual moments of my life. I can even tell you exactly where I was standing. It was so incredibly powerful. I spoke honestly and openly with my Creator. To me, the whole camp was worth that one moment when I deepened my relationship with G-d.

Prayer, as I mentioned on Rosh Hashana, is not limited to shul and it's not limited to Hebrew. Talk to G-d. Pour out your heart to Him. Develop a real relationship with your Creator. The most straightforward and meaningful way to bring G-d into our lives is by talking to Him, by inviting Him into our lives, into our moments of joy and our struggles.

I began with a story from Rabbi Levi Yitzchak of Berditchev and I'll finish with one. The story goes that he was once walking through the town, when he heard a little girl crying. He walked over to her to see what was wrong. She explained, "I was playing hide and go seek with my friends. I went to go hide and I waited for them to find me. I waited and waited and waited. Finally I realized that they stopped looking for me! There I was, hiding, and no one was looking for me!" And she continued to cry.

Rav Levi Yitzchak listened to her and then burst out crying himself. That obviously made the girl stop crying. "Rabbi, why are you crying?"

And he told her, "Young girl, you're in good company. G-d created this world and then He hid inside the world. The purpose of hiding was so that we could find Him. G-d also cries because it seems like no one's looking for Him anymore."

Let's look for G-d! Let's talk about G-d! Let's remind ourselves that everything we have and do is a gift from G-d. Let's remind ourselves and our families that everything that happens to us is the hand of G-d. As a nation, let's see the forest for the trees. Again, do not to give up on whatever causes we are most passionate about, but always remember what Judaism is really about – G-d! In our own lives, let's create a dialogue with our Creator, our Father, our King.

These ten days between Rosh Hashana and Yom Kippur are a time that we are supposed to recognize that G-d is our King and our Father, and that He runs the world. Let's do exactly that. Let's proclaim, not in a loud voice, but in a soft one, that *Ad-nai hu haElokim*, that G-d is in this world. He *is* in our lives. All we have to do is open our eyes and find Him.

Sermon sponsored by
Jonathan & Deborah Hamburger

WE DEDICATE THIS SERMON TO THE ROLE MODELS IN OUR LIVES.

To our parents, Theodore and Beverly Hamburger and Marshall and Sheila Cohen whose support and devotion to family and community continue to inspire us and our children.

And to Rabbi Yisrael and Hindy Motzen whose transformational leadership has energized and inspired the entire Baltimore community and beyond.

WHAT IF?

THE YEAR: 1712 BCE. THE GREAT KING AND JUDGE HAMMURABI HAS DIED. His son Samsu-iluna attempts to hold together his father's sprawling Babylonian Empire. He proves unsuccessful; instead, the order carefully constructed by his father crumbles into chaos.

Across the Euphrates lives a man, known by many as an eccentric. He claims to speak to G-d – not just any G-d, but an abstract G-d, one Who takes no physical form, cannot be seen, and makes promises long into the future. Despite his radical claims, this man is widely respected – he is powerful, wealthy, and exceptionally kind. He is known to treat every stranger with love, every passerby as if they're family. While nearby Babylon is burning, descending into anarchy, Avraham our patriarch, Avraham Avinu, is preaching a message of justice and peace, of love and life. He preaches not of a G-d in whom man must believe, but in a G-d who believes in man.

One night, deep in sleep, Avraham beholds a vision. This is nothing out of the ordinary; he has had many prophetic visions. But this is different. It is a violent vision of coldblooded murder, in which G-d commands him to take his beloved son and bring him as an offering. Child sacrifice.

He wakes up in a cold sweat. His beloved wife is sleeping soundly next to him. He recalls their struggles and their journey. How they left the comfort of their home to pursue his visions. How they encountered adversity at every step of the way. How their relationship was tried and tested through their childlessness. How they somehow, miraculously, had a child at an exceptionally old age. All of that comes crashing down with the words: "Take your child, the one you love, and bring him up as an offering."

It must have been a nightmare, not a vision from his loving G-d! Avraham closes his eyes and tries to fall back asleep.

But sleep eludes him. He cannot sleep.

And so he slips out of bed, making sure not to wake his wife Sara, and he quietly awakens his beloved son, Yitzchak. With tears in his eyes he whispers, "We need to go."

They travel for three days in absolute silence.

Yitzchak knows something is terribly wrong. He knows his father is in deep turmoil, and he has a dreadful, foreboding sense that it has to do with him. After all, if they're going to bring sacrifices, as the firewood and sharp knife seem to indicate, "Where is the lamb" that is to be slaughtered?

But Yitzchak is silent, respectful, stoic.

Each night, they set up a makeshift campsite. Yitzchak quickly falls asleep, tired from a day of traveling. But Avraham cannot sleep. He tosses and turns. He is physically and emotionally drained, but paralyzing fear overwhelms his body, preventing it from drifting into sleep. "Did I really hear G-d say what I think He said?" "Maybe it was just a dream?" "Maybe this has all been one long dream! Maybe everyone back home was right. Maybe" – he can't believe he is even considering it – "but maybe G-d does not exist. Maybe my mind was just playing tricks with me. Maybe it's time to turn around and go home. Sara must be so worried…"

And then that voice is countered with another, a whisper; "*What if?*" What if G-d *does* exist? What if G-d really *did* create this world? What if G-d really *did* imbue me with a soul and with a purpose? What if G-d wants me to do something with my life? *What if?*

So Avraham forges ahead.

The midrashim teach us that every moment of Avraham's journey to Mt. Moriah was filled with internal debate: was this all just a big mistake?

After all, Avraham's belief in G-d led to some pretty uncomfortable conclusions. Uncomfortable physically: personally I'm afraid of getting a shot at the doctor, yet Avraham circumcised himself at the age of 99. Uncomfortable emotionally: he was alienated from his entire family. And ultimately, his belief in G-d took him within a step of slaughtering his own son.

It would have been far more comfortable for him to just imagine that it was all a dream. Just like it's far more comfortable to ignore the nagging feeling that something is lacking in our lives. It's far more comfortable to continue on, doing the exact same things we've always done. It's far more comfortable to stop questioning our life trajectory once we graduate from college or we get married or buy a house. You know what it would mean to rethink my life right now?

But *what if*. What if it's real. What if it's true?

What if all this is more than just tradition and rituals and apple cake for dessert?

What if G-d did speak to our great-great-great-grandparents and gave them a moral code, a set of laws to live their life by? Like, for real. Not just something to tell our children at the Pesach Seder.

What if G-d expects something of us? Not just a general-fuzzy-be-a-better-person-and-light-unto-the-nations type of expectation, but in a very particular fashion, with daily prayer, Torah study, *lashon hara*, and kosher. *What if*?

I'm not sure if I'm supposed to say this out loud, but it's true, so I will. I have asked myself if G-d exists. More often than not, I know He does. More often than not, I think about the incredible world around me, about the miracle of Jewish continuity, about the wonders of creation and there is no question. More often than not, I feel like I am talking to some Being as I stand in prayer. And I just know.

But I have wondered. I have wondered if it's all a game that I was born into, if it's all just a fable that has kept our people alive. I have wondered if my decisions really make a difference. If there's really any purpose.

Those moments, I should add, are rather scary, rather dark, for they imply that I've dedicated my life to a fairytale – a pretty dark thought.

In those dark moments of doubt, invariably, another voice in my head responds with two words: *What if?*

There is very little that we know for certain. From the early days of the Enlightenment and on, we have questioned every one of our religious dogmas. In our 21st-century world of fake news and alternative facts, we have become even more skeptical, and for good reason. So I cannot prove to you, or tell you definitively, that G-d exists. But *what if*? What if He does?

We're all going to pray in just a few moments. How many of us really truly believe in what we're going to say?

The great 15th-century philosopher Rav Yosef Albo explains that the three blessings in Mussaf correspond to the three most fundamental Jewish beliefs.

The first section, that of *Malchuyyos*, speaks to G-d being our King. We are proclaiming that He created the world and controls it.

The section of *Zichronos* proclaims that G-d is aware of everything we do. Nothing escapes His attention.

And in the section of *Shofaros* we proclaim that we believe that the shofar was blown at Mt. Sinai, and that G-d gave us a set of laws by which He expects us to live our lives.

Do we believe any of that? Do we think about that during our daily routine? How does our belief impact us when we make major and minor life decisions? Are we any different because of our faith?

We like the tunes, we like the comforting feel of our seat, surrounded by our family and friends. *But what if this was all real*? What would that mean practically? Not just for the rest of this morning. What would it mean practically beyond the here and now?

Probably, a lot.

If G-d really existed, and G-d really knew what we are thinking, watched our actions, and wanted us to do something very specific with our lives, and if we don't there will be consequences, our lives would look different, wouldn't they?

That's a very uncomfortable thought. So uncomfortable that I should probably pivot to a heartwarming story right now. But I won't.

It's okay to be uncomfortable from time to time. Let's just sit, or squirm for a moment with the possibility that G-d is real, the Torah is true, and that there really is a court case taking place right now, reviewing our record in light of the Torah's commandments. And that if we are honest with ourselves, we're probably not doing so well.

All the things we said this year that we shouldn't have said.

All the things we did this year that we shouldn't have done.

And all the many missed opportunities. All the days, weeks, and months wasted – in pursuit of what?

Let's just sit with that for a moment.

Now the truth is, there is another possibility, but I find it to be equally uncomfortable, if not more so. It's a possibility that Avraham grappled with many years before the Binding of Isaac. It's a possibility that was taken for granted on the other side of the Euphrates back at home, in the ancient Mesopotamian world. A different what if: What if that loving G-d does *not* exist? What if my life has no intrinsic meaning whatsoever? What if this really is all meaningless?

This is how writer/blogger/philosopher, Mark Manson puts it:

"If I worked at Starbucks," he writes, "instead of writing people's names on their coffee cup, I'd write the following":

One day, you and everyone you love will die. And beyond a small group of people for an extremely brief period of time, little of what you say or do will ever matter. This is the Uncomfortable Truth of life. And everything you think or do is but an elaborate avoidance of it. We are inconsequential cosmic dust, bumping and milling about on a tiny blue speck. We imagine our own importance. We invent our purpose—we are nothing.

Enjoy your coffee."

You see, neither of these what-ifs end well. The inherently meaningful world of a G-d, a soul, a set of rules and expectations, is terribly overbearing. And the meaningless world without a purpose or Creator, of pure biology, and of arbitrary codes of conduct, is terribly depressing.

But instead of thinking and choosing, we drink our caramel macchiato – complaining about the lack of plastic straws, of course – while we scroll to the next email, message, or Facebook post. We ignore this dilemma, don't we? We distract ourselves from these uncomfortable possibilities of existence, because who in the world wants to think about that?

Or we do something even better. Something far more sophisticated. You and I. That's right, you and I, in shul, this Rosh Hashana morning. We're very clever. This is what we do:

You and I have just enough spirituality, tradition, faith, and meaning in our lives to escape the depressing thought of being cosmic dust. But not too much spirituality, tradition, faith, and meaning to make our lives too difficult. A little bit of sacrifice makes me feel good, too much and I'm getting heartburn. "I don't want to be a fanatic." We're clever, aren't we?

In a TED talk viewed by almost 3 million people, Swiss philosopher Alain de Botton proposed what he described as Atheism 2.0. Its starting point is a disbelief in G-d, but he suggests that this disbelief should not preclude one from borrowing what is good in religion. You got that? He's an atheist, so he does not believe in G-d, but he wants to take what is good from religion. In his words:

I'm interested in the kind of constituency that thinks something along these lines – that thinks, "I can't believe in any of this stuff. I can't believe in the doctrines. I don't think these doctrines are right. But… I love Christmas carols. I really like the art of Mantegna. I really like looking at old churches. I like turning the pages of the Old Testament."

Whatever it may be, you know the kind of thing I'm talking about – people who are attracted to the ritualistic side, the moralistic, communal side of religion, but can't bear the doctrine. Until now, these people have faced a rather unpleasant choice. It's almost as though either you accept the doctrine and then you can have all the nice stuff, or you reject the doctrine and you're living in some kind of spiritual wasteland under the guidance of CNN and Walmart.

He goes on to suggest that atheists adopt what he considers to be the good things in religion, things like a calendar and rituals that remind us of important values. Art and music that is not art for art's sake. Art that is meant to move people in one way or another. An educational model that is more than just sharing information, instead assuming that people need help and guidance. And my favorite: sermons. He suggests that atheists need more sermons. Go figure.

And as I'm listening to his talk, I'm thinking: *this isn't atheism 2.0, this is religion 2.0! It's what we do!*

If we were honest with ourselves, isn't our religion, the Judaism that we practice just a mashup of a bunch of Jewish cultural components that make us feel good? How much of what we do is driven by faith and how much of what we do is driven by comfort? This is what I'm used to. This is what my friends do. This is what I've always done.

And this is true, by the way, whether you drove here today or walked, whether you have a *sheitel* on your head or a *kippa* that keeps on slipping off, whether you were born into this lifestyle or you've taken leaps and bounds to get here. We should all ask: how much of our Jewish life *today* is intentional and how much of our Jewish life is a product of habit? How much of our Jewish day-to-day living is about G-d and how much of our Jewish life is about us?

G-d doesn't only care about how many *mitzvot* you are performing on a daily basis. Judaism is not a point system or a diet. (It's definitely not a diet!)

He wants us to be connected to Him, to have a relationship with Him. Do we believe in Him? Are we seeking a personal connection with Hashem? Do we believe the Torah is true? Do we believe G-d sees us and cares? Because if we did, if we *really* did, if we were really honest with ourselves, I don't think any of us would live the life we are currently living.

* * *

Our tradition teaches us that when Avraham was a young man he was arrested and given a mock trial. He was accused of planting dangerous seeds of rebellion against the establishment with his radical ideas of monotheism. After a quick decision by a kangaroo court, Avraham was given a choice: renounce his beliefs and state publicly that he was mistaken or burn at the stake. Avraham, with his head held high, publicly reaffirmed his belief in a kind and loving G-d. Our tradition teaches us that Avraham was thrown into a fiery pit and was miraculously saved.

Less well-known is that the same midrashic passage informs us that Avraham had a brother named Chur. Right before Avraham was thrown into the fiery pit, the judges asked Chur, "What about you? Do you believe in the monotheistic G-d of Avraham, or are you a polytheist like the rest of us?"

Chur told the judge that he needed to think about it; he'll let him know *after* Avraham was thrown into the fire pit. Chur was clever. Maybe a little too clever.

After Avraham emerged from the fiery pit unscathed, Chur loudly announced that he too was a believer in G-d. So they threw him in the fire. And he died.

Life is too precious, too fleeting, too short to hedge our bets. Are you an atheist? Be an atheist. Are you a believer? Be a believer. The message of the midrash is clear: you cannot be both. Whatever path you choose, choose it fully, as uncomfortable as it may be.

* * *

It was a brilliantly clear day in Jerusalem. Avraham, ready to collapse from exhaustion, tied his beloved son to the altar they had built together. With tears pouring from his eyes, Avraham lifted the knife, ready to fulfill the will of G-d. And G-d said, "Stop!" "You have proven yourself. *You do believe in G-d.*"

In Yitzchak's place, Avraham brought a ram, whose horn we blow every Rosh Hashana. That ram's horn, which we will blow in just a moment, is a reminder of Avraham's deep and unyielding faith. As we hear its sound, listen closely. It will be asking us one simple question. A question that needs to be answered by every one of us, every day of our lives:

What if?

Sermon Sponsored by the Ner Tamid Sisterhood

THE NER TAMID SISTERHOOD IS HUMBLY GRATEFUL FOR THE CONSISTENT support of our dynamic duo, Rabbi and Rebbetzin Motzen. Through the advice and direct involvement (big shoutout to member Rebbetzin Hindy!) in the planning as well as the execution stages of our endeavors, the Motzens guide and sustain the Sisterhood's goals to the benefit of our kehillah and greater community. They assist in making our work spiritually uplifting and socially successful. Their energies are magnetic and meaningful, and we are deeply appreciative of their guidance and participation in our work.

Todah Rabbah!

THOSE WHO CHOOSE TO STAY

There is a video on YouTube called the Awareness Test. It begins with a group of people standing around and a voiceover asking you to count how many times the ball will be passed from one person to another. They start passing the ball. They're moving quickly and it's a bit difficult to keep track. But while this is happening, a person in a full-length gorilla outfit moonwalks across the screen. Most people, including myself, miss it entirely. We're so focused on counting how many times the ball is passed that we completely miss something as glaring as a gorilla dancing across the screen.

I was thinking about this video as I read through this week's parsha. The bulk of our Torah portion, Chayei Sarah, describes how Avraham's servant, Eliezer, finds a suitable marriage partner for Yitzchak. It describes how Avraham gives instructions to Eliezer, how he travels to the land of Padan Aram leading donkeys laden with gold, silver, and jewelry, how he prays to G-d to assist him, how he finds a suitable match, Rivka, how he has to persuade Rivka's family to have her come with him, and finally, how he returns to Yitzchak. *Sixty-seven verses* describing the very first matchmaking tale in Jewish history. Why is so much ink spilled over this tale?

The classic answer to this question is offered by the Midrash. It suggests that the unique length of this episode encourages us to study the text carefully so we can glean lessons from Eliezer's faith, wisdom, and tenacity. The great detail is there because not only are our forefathers incredible models, but even their servants have what to teach us.

But something else occurred to me this year, of which I subsequently found a version in the Sefas Emes: *there is a gorilla walking across this screen.* I have been so busy watching Eliezer that I didn't notice the intense drama playing out right before my eyes.

You see, there is another Midrash that wonders why Avraham forces Eliezer to take an oath that he would find a wife for Yitzchak from Padan Aram. Eliezer is his employee, and you don't typically ask your employee to take an oath. "Swear to me that you will get me that report by the end of the week! Take an oath!" It's strange. The Midrash suggests that there was some underlying tension in this interaction. Eliezer was committed to Avraham and Sarah. He dedicated his life to them and their cause. He fought with Avraham against the four kings, traveled with Avraham to the *Akeda*, and he himself was circumcised. He was so dedicated that at one point, before Avraham had any children of his own, Avraham thought Eliezer would be the next leader of the nation that he was forming. Of course, once Yitzchak was born it became clear that Eliezer would not be the successor.

But not all was lost. Eliezer had a daughter – a special, kind, thoughtful, spiritual daughter, who was well-versed in Avraham's way of life. Like her father, she was dedicated to the cause. Eliezer had spent the last decades assuming his daughter would marry Yitzchak. He held off on marrying her to anyone else, knowing that she was destined for greatness.

And then, one day, Avraham calls Eliezer into his tent and says that he wants to speak about Yitzchak. *This is it! Finally! I will take my rightful place in the development of this new and wonderful nation!* But instead, Avraham instructs Eliezer to travel to another country, to find a woman they don't even know, that his daughter has no chance of marrying Yitzchak. And all his dreams come crashing down.

Avraham senses Eliezer's disappointment. Avraham is concerned that Eliezer, wealthy, shrewd, and knowing that his master, Avraham, doesn't have much longer to live, may manipulate the situation. So he makes Eliezer take an oath that he'll follow through with his instructions.

And now, with that understanding in mind, read the next sixty-seven verses and tell me, do you now hear a thousand nails scratching on a chalkboard? Do you now sense the weight that Eliezer is carrying? Do you now appreciate how at every turn, Eliezer could have and maybe should have taken the donkeys filled with gold and silver and walked off into the sunset? Think about the disappointment, the frustration, the rejection that he must have felt.

Yet he carried on. He put on a brave face. He fought against every feeling in his body. Despite the heartbreak he had to deal with at every step of the journey, he went forward with poise, faith, and joy, and ultimately returned to Avraham.

That's why the story goes on and on. The Torah wants us to feel the intense emotion that is bubbling up right beneath the surface. The Torah wants us to open our eyes not only to Eliezer's invisible pain but to the invisible pain that so many carry and struggle with each day. And perhaps most importantly, the Torah wants to present a role model for the many people who will need Eliezer to look up to – for the people in our communities who feel rejected, dismayed, and ignored, and through him will somehow find the strength to carry on.

I recently read a book called *Unmatched*. It's a well-written memoir by an Orthodox Jewish woman describing her attempt to get married. It's raw, funny, insightful, and terribly sad. The author is smart, accomplished, funny, thoughtful, and attractive, yet she is consistently set up with bozos. There was the guy who made her travel across New York for a date and showed up forty-five minutes late even though he lived a block away. There was the guy who kept on making physical advances on her, which she rejected because of her observance, only to be dropped by him because "she was not religious enough for him." There was the guy who started the date by looking her up and down and saying, "You're not very pretty." There was the guy who came to the first date with a list of a hundred questions on which he drilled her. There was the guy who kept on reaching out to her to talk and hang out but was consistently dating others at the same time. There was the guy who slammed the door in her face upon meeting her. And on and on and on.

And while she continued to date dud after dud, she was bombarded by friends, rabbis, and strangers: "You're too old. You're too ugly. Are you straight? Why don't you do this? Why don't you do that?" She received endless attention from her community, but only about her singlehood. Her interests, successful career, and talents all went unnoticed. She lived in the Jewish community, attended shul and social functions, and greeted her neighbors every morning, but felt utterly rejected and ignored. The explosive pain of rejection – by friends, rabbinic leaders, and, most hurtful, G-d – was invisible to anyone who interacted with her, but it was hidden right beneath the surface.

Like Eliezer, she should have run. But like Eliezer, she stayed firmly put. And that's what moved me most of all in this book. She never ran. She never let go. Sure, she slipped. She did things that were beneath her standards. She flirted with ideas that would have taken her well out of our faith. But ultimately, she held on.

Reading *Unmatched* made me appreciate just how many such people we have in our midst. Whether it's people who are single, divorcees, widows, people who have been through a tragedy and did not receive the support they needed from their community, people who have been abused and did not feel that they were believed, people who due to their orientation or any other reason we're made to feel like outcasts, there are no shortage of gorillas moonwalking all around us. Only that they're not gorillas; they're human beings. And they're not moonwalking; they're falling apart.

And yet, like Eliezer, such people are here in our community, in this shul. They somehow hold on.

By describing the story of Eliezer in such detail, G-d is trying to wake us up to the Eliezers in our midst, to open our eyes and be more attuned to pain that we may not be able to appreciate. By utilizing sixty-seven verses, G-d is conveying to us that He can see beneath the surface, that He sees that pain, that He cares. But most importantly, by taking so much space up in our precious Torah, G-d is conveying to us how heroic such an existence really is. To practice a way of life that seems to not fit with your life circumstances; to live in a community that is not always attuned to your needs; to engage with a G-d who seems, at times, as if He is out to get you – that is a story worthy of all the holy ink in the world.

The book concludes – spoiler alert – with the woman in her 50s, still 'unmatched.' She writes:

We are stronger than we think. We come from a chain of strong women starting with our own mothers and grandmothers, going all the way back to our Biblical foremothers and all the ordinary Jewish women throughout history who faced extraordinary challenges and met them with bravery and faith.

Perhaps wider society ridicules and casts us as pathetic. Perhaps those who are happily married would never choose to trade places with us. But we are ordinary women doing something very extraordinary. Each time we put our faith before ourselves, each time we hold on to G-d rather than turn away, we are erecting another spiritual skyscraper unequalled by any of the wonders of the world.

We are *unmatched*. We are strong. This is our challenge, and we will meet it.

Sermon Sponsored by Naftali Topas

THIS SERMON IS DEDICATED IN MEMORY OF MY BELOVED BROTHER, MOSHE Aharon ben Matisyahu Yaakov. Moshe's ability to connect with everyone he met and to be there for people when they needed him is a testament to the generous man he was.

May the learning of these divrei Torah by Rabbi Motzen bring Moshe an aliyas neshama.

THE LIMITATIONS OF
#THANK YOU HASHEM

A FEW MONTHS AGO, I WAS RIDING THE AMTRAK TRAIN FROM NEW YORK to Baltimore, sitting by myself and talking on the phone, when someone approached me, trying to hand me something. My immediate assumption was that the man was a Christian missionary. Who else gives things out to people – especially to Jews? I finally looked down at what he had in his hand and saw that it was a chazzanus CD. I assumed the man might have known of my father; I wasn't quite sure. I took the CD and motioned that as soon as I got off the phone, I would come over to him.

A few minutes later, I sat down with the man, who introduced himself as Zev. He was a philanthropist who had just commissioned a Conservative synagogue in New York to create a CD with cantorial music. We chatted for a little while: I told him about our shul, he told me about what he does, and that was it.

About a week later, I received a letter from Zev with a check for $100. "So nice," I thought to myself. This is not his shul; does not go to an ortho-dox synagogue, and does not live in Baltimore, but this man is clearly very thoughtful and classy. So I sent him a message thanking him for his generosity.

A month later, I received a letter in the mail, this time with $50 cash, telling me to use it for my family for Chanuka. Now this was over the top. I barely knew the man and now he was giving me Chanuka gifts. This time I picked up the phone to thank him. While we were schmoozing, he told me his foundation was about to give some major gifts, so I figured I'd tell him about some things happening in our shul that could use sponsorship, hoping that maybe we would receive one of those gifts. I shared a project or two with him and waited to see how he would respond. After a long pause, he said, "I'll be honest, none of these projects really speak to me or our foundation.

However, I really appreciated how you called me to thank me. Not enough people do that. I'll send you something."

Two weeks later, I opened a letter from Zev to find a check for $10,000. (We subsequently found something that was in line with his foundation and directed the funds to that project.)

Now let me ask you a question. Was my being on that train a coincidence or not? If I remember correctly, I was actually scheduled to take a different train, and I changed my ticket at the last minute. Was the fact that I was on that train, two rows behind Zev, pure chance or was it divinely ordained?

Most people with whom I shared this story said, "It was bashert," the Yiddish word for something predestined. Others would say it was a sign of *hashgacha peratis*, personal divine providence. *Hashgacha peratis* is the belief that everything that happens to us is divinely orchestrated, that there are no coincidences.

Sometimes we realize it – such as when we receive a check in the mail for $10,000 – and sometimes we don't. But it's always there. The Ramban (Shemos 13:16), in explaining why we constantly review the story of the Exodus from Egypt, writes beautifully how through the open miracles of the Ten Plagues, we are supposed to open our eyes to the endless *hidden* miracles that take place every moment.

This belief in what I would call extreme *hashgacha peratis*, how every single occurrence in my life is arranged by G-d, is part of the everyday education of our sons and daughters. They will be bombarded with beautiful stories of apparent mishaps that turn out to be blessings. Stories like people missing planes on 9/11 and the like.

Most recently, a mini-movement has developed, known as Thank You Hashem. It promotes precisely this idea: that no matter what happens to us, we need to say, "thank you Hashem." You may have seen their bumper stickers, #TYH, or countless other forms of TYH swag; they even make TYH jewelry. They composed a song titled – you guessed it – "Thank You Hashem."

The music video is filled with people losing their jobs or experiencing other mishaps, but learning to nonetheless say, "Thank You Hashem!"

Beautiful! No? What could possibly be wrong with more gratitude and more G-d-awareness?

Let me tell you another story. My wife was once speaking to a young woman who was really struggling. It turned out that this young woman was once sexually violated, which she was obviously grappling with. Compounding her pain was a question, why did G-d want this to happen to me? What did I do wrong such that I was deserving of this terrible punishment?

You see, if I believe in extreme *hashgacha peratis*, that every single thing that happens to us is a result of G-d pulling the strings, then just like G-d wanted me to sit down next to a future friend and donor of Ner Tamid, G-d also wanted this horrific violation to happen to me. I must be a terrible person. I must be scum of the earth. G-d must hate me. Why else would He do this to me? Faced with this predicament, I can imagine the Thank You Hashem theme song screeching to a halt.

I was very moved by this young woman's ordeal and her theological dilemma. I penned a little dark poem in response:

#ThankYouHashem for returning my precious soul
#ThankYouHashem for making me so whole
#ThankYouHashem for new opportunities each day
#ThankYouHashem for friends and family You have sent my way

#ThankYouHashem for making me so ill
#ThankYouHashem for depression, anxiety, and pills
#ThankYouHashem for loneliness each night
#ThankYouHashem for abusing me; I'm traumatized for life

There is a dark side to this belief of personalized divine providence. I imagine that some, if not many of you, have experienced this question on some level: why did G-d do this to me? Why is G-d punishing me?

The truth is that many great Jewish philosophers rejected this idea of extreme *hashgacha peratis*. They argued that of course G-d is *able* to orchestrate anything; after all, G-d is Omnipotent. But He most often does not intervene in this way. The Ten Plagues, according to this view, are the exception, not the rule. Yes, there is justice – we will be rewarded for our good deeds, punished for the bad – but for the most part, not in this world. Justice will take place in the next world. And yes, G-d *can* intervene – that is the premise of prayer, asking G-d to change nature – but for the most part, He does not. He allows nature to run its course.

Following this second view of how G-d manages the world, when something happens to us, good or bad, it's nature. G-d did not, heaven forbid, want you to be violated. G-d did not want you to be ill. G-d created a world with the capacity for evil, with the capacity for illness, and for the most part, He stands back and allows nature to do its thing: the good, the bad, and the ugly. And again, to emphasize, G-d is cognizant of what is taking place on earth, but the way He set things up is that He does not regularly intervene.

When my wife shared this second approach with the young woman she was speaking to, her entire sense of self changed. You mean this was not a punishment from G-d? You mean I have every right to be furious at the man who did this to me? You mean G-d does care about me, and, like a parent, at times, makes the incredibly difficult decision to stand back? Yes, yes, and yes.

Rav Yehuda Halevi, a twelfth-century poet and scholar, in his magnum opus, the *Kuzari*, presents both views. He demonstrates the pros and cons of each one, delineating philosophical and textual challenges to each one of these perspectives. He concludes with a pragmatic approach: It may be best to assume that everything comes from Hashem, but it's really not so clear that this is the case. At the very least, assume that the big things in life come from G-d and take them to heart. The small things, not so much. (Kuzari, 5:20)

If he's not willing to weigh in with certainty, I surely will not do so either. I can't tell you which view is right. I cannot tell you how to live your life – whether everything that happens is from G-d or everything, or most things that happen, are coincidences. I will leave that to you, to think about, to discuss, to debate. A sermon does not give us enough time to discuss this incredibly weighty topic properly.

But I do want to leave you with one definitive position. Wherever you land, on the side of extreme *hashgacha peratis* or with a more hands-off approach, there is one belief that both these approaches agree on and that I beg you to believe in as well. It's encapsulated in a two-line passage in a book called *Tzidkas Hatzadik*, which was written in the late nineteenth century by a man named Rav Tzadok Rabinowitz, otherwise known as Rav Tzadok Hakohen. He was a young prodigy, married into a very wealthy family, and was set to live a life of uninterrupted scholarship for the entirety of his life.

Unfortunately, things did not work out so well between him and his wife. He wanted to get divorced. She refused. He was forced to travel around Eastern Europe, penniless, with nothing to his name. He never had children and spent most of his life completely unknown.

In the 154th chapter of *Tzidkas HaTzadik* he writes, "*Kesheim shetzarich adam leha'amin baHashem Yisborach,* Just as a person must believe in Hashem, *kach*, with the same level of belief, with the same intensity, *tzarich leha'amin be'atzmo*, a person must believe in themselves. *Ratza lomar*, meaning to say, *sheyeish laHashem Yisborach esek immo*, Hashem cares about you... *shenafsho mimekor Hachaim*, that one's soul is from the Source of all holiness, *vaHashem Yisborach misaneig umishtashei'a bah keshe'oseh retzono*, and G-d takes incredible delight when we fulfill His will."

Whether our life is orchestrated by G-d down to the very detail or whether what is happening to us is simply nature running its course, G-d cares. A lot. About you. About me. About each of us. He is there, watching us, rooting us on, crying when we're in pain.

Personally, I struggle with the #TYH bandwagon. But that doesn't mean that I cannot say thank you, Hashem. My version, based on that teaching of Rav Tzadok, would sound something like this. This is the conclusion of the poem I wrote:

#ThankYouHashem for holding me when I am ill
#ThankYouHashem for understanding me when no else will
#ThankYouHashem for loving me despite my many flaws
#ThankYouHashem for life; with all its gifts and all its loss

Section III –

JUDAISM TODAY

Sermon Sponsored by Nina and Steve Ungar

IN HONOR OF RABBI AND REBBETZIN MOTZEN FOR ALL THE INSPIRING MES-
sages given over the years to help lift up and center the kehillah. To many,
many more years to come.

ISRAEL AT 75

I'D LIKE TO SHARE WITH YOU A STORY OF ONE OF OUR GREATEST TEACHERS, Nachmanides, also known as Ramban (an acronym of Rabbi Moshe ben Nachman, and not to be confused with Rambam, Rabbi Moshe ben Maimon). Ramban was born in Spain in 1194 and was a physician by trade. He was best-known for authoring brilliant commentaries on the Chumash and the Talmud, and for the philosophical and mystical ideas he incorporated throughout his writings.

This was still centuries before the Inquisition, but anti-Jewish sentiment was growing in Spain. One technique used by the Church was to "prove Judaism wrong" by holding a religious debate known as a disputation between a rabbi and a priest. Such undertakings were fraught with danger. If the rabbi lost, Jews would be forced to convert. If the rabbi won, things weren't necessarily any better. After one disputation, for example, despite the fact that the rabbi had won the debate, copies of the Talmud were burned by the cartload.

In 1263, King James I of Aragon authorized a disputation between Nachmanides and a Jewish convert to Christianity, Pablo Christiani. Nachmanides reluctantly agreed to take part only after being assured by the King that he would have full freedom of expression. King James, who had a complicated relationship with the Church, agreed.

According to some sources, Nachmanides won the battle but lost the war. His arguments earned the King's respect and a prize of 300 gold coins, but the Church ordered Nachmanides to be tried on the charge of blasphemy. A friend tipped him off and so, in the middle of the night, Nachmanides, who was roughly 73 at the time, fled his homeland never to return.

After a long and perilous journey, Nachmanides arrived at the port city of Akko. He had decided to make *aliyya*. After a brief stay, he traveled to Yerushalayim, where he was struck by its desolation. Buildings were dilapidated and abandoned. There were so few Jews that he could not even find ten men for a minyan. In a letter to his son, he wrote:

> What can I tell you about the land? There are so many forsaken places, and the desecration is great. The more sacred the place, the greater the devastation it has suffered. Yerushalayim is the most desolate place of all!

I imagine Nachmanides standing there in Israel, thousands of miles from his homeland, knowing that he would never see his family again. He realized that the golden era of Jewish life in Spain was slowly coming to an end. The future looked bleak. And he came to the Promised Land, described in the Torah as overflowing with milk and honey. Instead, what met his eyes was utter desolation.

And yet, amazingly, Nachmanides remained hopeful. He recalled a passage in the Torah, in what is known as the *Tochecha*, in which G-d describes the terrible suffering the Jewish people would endure. The Land of Israel during this period of exile is described as follows:

> So devastated will I leave the land, that your enemies who live there will be astonished... *Your land will remain desolate* and your cities in ruins. (Vayikra 26:32-33)

In his commentary to the Chumash – which he may have begun writing upon his arrival in Yerushalayim – Nachmanides explained that the words, "Your land will remain desolate," which appear in the middle of a string of curses, are actually a blessing to the Jewish people. That verse, he argued in a fantastically creative leap from the simple text, was actually a reassurance from G-d. As he put it:

That which G-d states here, "Your land will remain desolate," constitutes a good tiding, proclaiming that during all our exiles our land will not accept our enemies. This is a great proof and assurance to us, for in the entire inhabited world one cannot find such a good and large land which was always lived in, and yet is as ruined as it is [today]. For since the time that we left it, it has not accepted any nation or people, and they all try to settle it, but to no avail.

He had a good point. Throughout the many centuries since the Jewish people were exiled from their land, no conqueror succeeded in permanently settling the land. For 2,000 years, Israel remained a wasteland. As Mark Twain wrote in the late nineteenth century, "A desolation is here that not even imagination can grace with the pomp of life and action."

Somehow, in the ruins of Yerushalayim, Nachmanides saw a fulfillment of G-d's promise that the land was waiting for the Jews to return. He understood that the destruction of the land was an incredible testimony to the bond between G-d and His people. He saw in the barren wasteland a living proof that G-d had not forsaken us. G-d made a promise to us and He would keep it.

On the one hand, G-d seemed so distant and removed from the world. The dark clouds of the Inquisition were beginning to descend over his native land. The temptation to convert was stronger than ever. And yet, Nachmanides saw through the Land of Israel that G-d was sending him and all the Jewish people a message: "I am not that far away." If one listened closely enough, with a sensitive ear like that of Ramban, one could hear G-d whisper, ever so softly: "Look at this land! It makes no sense! How can a land that was so fruitful become such a wasteland? It's because I'm holding onto the land for you," said G-d. "I'm waiting for your return."

Ramban's tenacity and optimism are part of a long tradition. He was quite literally walking in the footsteps of another great sage who lived in Yerushalayim about a thousand years before him. The Talmud (Makkos 24b) relates that Rabbi Akiva was once walking through the ruins of Yerushalayim with his colleagues. They had witnessed the destruction of the Temple by the Romans, they had lived through fierce and bloody battles, and that morning, they found themselves walking near the Temple Mount – or should I say, the former Temple Mount. There was nothing. It was a razed field – a deliberate slap in the face by their Roman oppressors. And to add insult to injury, just as they walked by, a fox ran right over the space on which the Holy of Holies had once stood. The rabbis could not contain themselves, and they burst out into mournful crying. But Rabbi Akiva began to laugh. Shocked, they stopped crying, and asked him to explain himself. "Why are you laughing?"

"There is a verse in the book of Zecharia," he told them, "which speaks of foxes running through a desolate Jerusalem." They nodded their heads. "But there's another verse, this one in Yirmiyahu, in which Zecharia and another prophet by the name of Uriah are mentioned. Uriah's most famous prophecy is one we sing at weddings: "*Od yishama*," "we will yet hear in the cities of Judah… the voice of joy and happiness" (Yirmiyahu 33:10-11). Clearly, concluded Rabbi Akiva, there is meant to be a connection between the two. When the prophecy of Zecharia, that of foxes running through a desolate Yerushalayim, will be fulfilled, the uplifting prophecies of Uriah will be fulfilled as well! When we see foxes running through the Temple Mount, it is G-d's way of telling us that the prophecy of Uriah will also be fulfilled.

Did you follow that? A little convoluted, right? That's exactly my point. You see, for two thousand years, our greatest thinkers had to come up with the most creative leaps of faith, difficult, even stretched explanations to find hope in the desperate darkness. But today? In 2023? Who needs creativity? Who needs Talmudic reasoning?

If Nachmanides were to travel to Israel today, he wouldn't write home about destruction. He would probably write a letter to his son describing Tel Aviv. A hundred years ago, it was a patch of sand dunes, and it now boasts a population of just under half a million residents. He would describe Petach Tikva, at one point a swamp infected by malaria and now a flourishing city that doesn't stop growing. He would write about the economy that boasts the second-largest number of startup companies in the world after the United States, and the largest number of NASDAQ-listed companies outside of North America. He would describe a land overflowing with life and trees. Did you know that Israel exports tulips to Holland? That Israeli wine makers export to France?

At this point in history, you wouldn't need to be a Rabbi Akiva or a Ramban to interpret verses creatively. Anyone who owns a Chumash can open it up and see for themselves. Any one of us can open Yechezkel to read his crystal-clear prophecy from over 2,000 years ago: "Mountains of Israel shall give forth your branch and bear fruit for My people Israel" (36:8). Fulfilled in our days!

Any one of us can recall the prophecies of Yeshayahu, who described how G-d will one day gather Jews from all across the world: *"yekabetz mei'arba kanfos ha'aretz,"* "G-d will ingather [the Jewish People] from the four corners of the earth" (11:12). Every planeload of *olim* is a fulfilment of this promise!

G-d is no longer whispering to us that He has held on to His promise. He is shouting, loud and clear. That same land that was for so long forsaken, is now overflowing with milk and honey. I don't typically share miracle stories. They're not for me. I find my inspiration elsewhere. But the State of Israel is a miracle we cannot ignore.

I wish I could go back in time, to visit my great-grandparents right before they were gassed by the Nazis. I wish I could whisper to them what would happen in just a few years – the State of Israel would be born! Yerushalayim would be ours! *Har Habayit beyadeinu* – the Temple Mount would be in our hands! There would be a Jewish army – and they would be powerful! "How could it be?" they would ask. It's a miracle, they would shout. And they would be right.

For most of us, our great-grandparents and grandparents are no longer here. For some, it is parents who we are missing. How jealous would they be of us to be living at this time? And how would they respond?

For all the political instability, for all the truly unspeakable terror that we witnessed these past few days, we are living in miraculous times. *Hodu laShem ki tov!* For the State of Israel to have been born, *dayyeinu*. For the State of Israel to have reached seventy-five, there are no words to express the emotion for a miracle of such magnitude. So let's take a moment today, on this holiday of redemption, to appreciate the gift for which our ancestors yearned for 2,000 years. Let's take a moment today, on this holiday of thanksgiving, to thank G-d for what our ancestors had to imagine, and we can see with our own eyes. Let's take a moment today, on this holiday of hope, to be inspired by the hope of those who came before us, so that we merit to see not only *reshit tzemichat ge'ulateinu,* the messy beginnings of redemption, but the complete redemption speedily in our days. Amen!

Sermon Sponsored by
Anton and Tamara Samuel

MAZEL TOV TO RABBI AND REBBETZIN MOTZEN ON YOUR TEN-YEAR
anniversary!

THE GOLUS COMPLEX

In 1933, A LETTER WAS WRITTEN BY THE ORTHODOX JEWISH LEADERSHIP in Germany. It was addressed to the Chancellor of Germany, Adolf Hitler. The letter was a plea for safety and security, describing the terrible impact that the Nazi laws had caused the Jewish community and the fear in which they lived. In pleading their case, the rabbinic leadership, the authors of this letter, attempted to find common ground with the ruling party, the Nazis:

> Marxist materialism and Communist atheism share not the least in common with the spirit of the positive Jewish religious tradition, as handed down through Orthodox teachings obligatory on the Jewish people… We (too) have been at war against this religious attitude.

They went on to say that they would accept restrictions and laws that would limit their autonomy and opportunities. What they wanted was clarity: are the Nazis truly intent on removing Jews from the land, in which case they would leave, or are those just empty words, campaign slogans meant to curry votes that have no teeth to them, in which case they would happily reside in Germany as second-class citizens.

You could call the letter utterly naïve, or disgustingly reprehensible. With the benefit of hindsight, our judgment is likely unfairly harsh. What I can say definitively is that this position of the Jewish leadership was an expression of what is called a *golus* (exile) mentality, or what I would call a *golus* complex.

Some may blame this way of thinking, these rabbis' willingness to accept hateful rhetoric and discrimination, on 2,000 years of exile – living under Romans, Christians, and Muslims and being granted few rights and subject to regular pogroms, conditioned these leaders to think this way. But it goes back even further. Nachmanides, addressing the question of how it could be that the family of Yosef, the most powerful man in Egypt, could become slaves, suggests that it was not an overnight transformation. Rather, the Egyptians first started describing the Jewish people as vermin. Then, without taking an official policy, the ruling class encouraged – with words – the populace to attack the Jews. Eventually, they introduced legislation that discriminated against the Jews. And then they made them into slaves. Sounds familiar, doesn't it?

What would have happened had the Jews stood up for themselves at that very first stage and said, "We aren't vermin; we're human, just like you"? What would have happened had they spoken up when the peasants were attacking them? What would have happened had they lobbied against the discriminatory laws?

Who knows.

What we do know is that the few words we find in the mouths of those Jews in Egypt are words of apathy, of indifference, of preferring the predictable life of a slave over the challenging life of a free person. As Rav Mosheh Lichtenstein notes in his book *Tzir Vatzon*, when Moshe tries to rally the Jews to demand justice with his act of killing the Egyptian, they are apathetic to his cause and mock him. When Moshe tries to secure their freedom, the Jews push back at every stage.

Our *golus* complex goes back to before we were even a nation, and it lives with us still.

How is this complex expressed?

Our *golus* complex is expressed when we bicker over which form of antisemitism is worse: right-wing or left-wing, when no form of antisemitism should be acceptable to us.

Our *golus* complex is expressed when we choose candidates based exclusively on their relationship with Israel or the Jews and nothing else, completely losing sight of our *raison d'etre*, of being a light unto others, forgetting that our survival is not an end to itself but a means for the betterment of the world.

Our *golus* complex is expressed when we don't allow for honest report-ing of what goes on in our communities because we're afraid of a *shanda*, of a scandal or embarrassment to the Jewish people.

Our *golus* complex is expressed when we are so busy being defensive that we cannot extend ourselves to other "types" of Jews or to minorities who could use our support.

And like most pathologies, there are terrible inconsistencies.

On the one hand, we act like we are being endlessly persecuted, like we are complete strangers in this land. And at the very same time, we act like our ancestors came here on the Mayflower, and that there is no alternative to living in the USA.

On the one hand, we vote as if we are complete strangers in this land. And at the same time, we identify so deeply with our political party of choice that its leader becomes our prophet and its platform our creed. Yeshiva boys can quote Ben Shapiro but not Bava Basra, and Jewish Democrats would sooner criticize Moshe Rabbeinu than Barack Obama. Our political identity is such that rabbis are petrified to weigh in in any substantive way on the most pressing issues facing our nation because they'll alienate people who put politics before faith. And when religious leaders do weigh in, after the fact, and make a little tiny peep, it's heralded as heroic. That's a *golus* complex.

On the one hand we pray to return to our land three times a day. And at the same time, we build beautiful, over-the-top houses, we live lavish lifestyles, and we soak up the comforts of this country even when we can't afford them because Western materialism is so much a part of our Jewish culture. (Don't believe me? Read the ads in any Jewish publication, or just walk down the street.)

I sometimes wonder to myself: if the shofar of Mashiach would blow right now, would we really be able to pull ourselves away from our homes and move to Israel? Into a little two – or three-bedroom apartment? Without a brand-new Honda Odyssey?

If we're going to have a *golus* complex, let's at least be consistent! Let's keep a packed suitcase, stop rooting for the home team – they're not *our* team – and live like we're in exile.

* * *

Now it's very easy to diagnose a problem. It's far more difficult to suggest a solution. Unfortunately, I don't have a solution, but perhaps we can gain some inspiration from the very first *golus* (exile) and *geula* (redemption):

If we go back to the very first Pesach Seder, we notice something very strange: it was celebrated while the Jews were still living in Egypt. Pretty amazing, isn't it? They were living in their slave barracks in the land of their oppression, but they were celebrating *zeman cheiruseinu*, a holiday of freedom.

Freedom, it would seem, is not a location; *it's a state of mind*. And that night the Jews lived in a free state of mind. The message that G-d had conveyed to them through Moshe in this week's parsha finally penetrated:

"Hashem Elokei avoseichem nir'a eilay," "G-d, the G-d of our forefather, appeared to Moshe" – that they were the descendants of Avraham, Yitzchak, and Yaakov. And *"A'aleh eschem mei'ani Mitzrayim… el eretz zavas chalav udevash,"* "I will lift you up from Egypt and take you to a land flowing with milk and honey" – that they had a future. (Shemos 3:16-17)

That night they were reminded of their legacy: how Yaakov refused to make concessions or political partnerships with the likes of Esav and Lavan despite leaving himself vulnerable in the process. How Yitzchak was willing to give up everything, even his life, for the sake of G-d. And how Avraham cared not only for his own family, but for all the families of the world.

That night they were reminded of the future: how they did not belong in Egypt, how they had a calling, how they were to set up their own country, with their own set of laws, and how a light of ethics and morality would one day shine from Yerushalayim.

That night they were free. That night they broke off the shackles of that terrible complex.

* * *

You could live your whole life bound in chains, but unless you try to move around, you might not feel them. I imagine we all feel like we've been moved and shaken quite a lot this year, especially this past week. The President has been idolized by many in our community (you know, from the word, idol). We can have an honest discussion and debate about the best candidate for whom we should have voted. I truly believe that. But idolization? That's unacceptable. Despite the adoration, this past week, watching the capital of the country stormed caused many to feel a deep sense of fear, especially as Jews, even those with a limited knowledge of history. This past week we read "brave" op-eds and hushed whispers, wondering if maybe, just maybe, we were mistaken. Maybe he wasn't our savior. Maybe just maybe the idea that there will be a political savior for the Jewish people can never happen as long as we are in *golus*.

It's safe to say that right now, we are all awake to the fact that we are in chains. We suffer, as a people, in one way or another from a *golus* complex. The truth is, until that great shofar is blown, we will all be slaves, in Baltimore and even in Yerushalayim. But the process of freedom can begin, even here and especially now. By reminding ourselves of our legacy, of our values, and not pandering to whomever will hate us less, and by reminding ourselves of our calling and extending ourselves to all our neighbors. May G-d bless America, may He watch over this wonderful country which has treated us so well, and may we act in a way that brings blessing to the world.

Sermon Sponsored by The Ehrenfeld Family

IS JUDAISM RACIST?

I'LL BEGIN BY SAYING THAT THIS WILL BE A VERY LONG TALK. IT'S AN IMPORT-ant topic and therefore one that I would like to address honestly. Now of course, you should expect all topics that I discuss to be addressed honestly. But in perusing the World Wide Web, I think it's safe to say that most of the Jewish treatments of this topic are either polemics or apologetics. They either cherry-pick Torah sources or blatantly ignore them, making up ideas that are not found in the Torah.

I will be sharing sources, some with which we are more comfortable and others less so. I could just get up here and say, "Judaism does not believe in racism but some Jews are racist," and be done with it. But if we are going to have an honest conversation, let's be honest.

So, is Judaism racist? I believe the answer is, it depends and it depends.

It depends first and foremost on how you define racism. It also depends on which school of thought you identify with.

Let's begin with a definition of racism. According to the Oxford Dictionary, racism can be defined in two ways:

1) 1) "Prejudice, discrimination, or antagonism directed against someone of a different race based on the belief that one's own race is superior."

I do not believe that any Jewish source would endorse this form of racism. In fact, as we'll see, such racism would be prohibited on a number of counts.

But there's another, closely-related definition:

2) 2) "The belief that all members of each race possess characteristics, abilities, or qualities specific to that race especially so as to distinguish it as inferior or superior to another race or races."

This second definition maintains that races are different from one another, and possibly even superior by comparison. This a racial theory. The first definition involves acting out on those theories by discriminating against or antagonizing others. Obviously, there is a dangerously fine line between these two.

Bearing in mind these two working definitions, let's review the sources. Allow me to preface that there are many Jewish sources that say a lot of things. In our tradition, however, some have been accepted by mainstream authorities and other minority views have been relegated to the academic sphere. I will be sharing only classical, mainstream views.

The first is that of the Rambam. In the final section of the *Laws of Shemitta and Yovel*, he writes the following moving statement:

כל איש ואיש מכל באי העולם אשר נדבה רוחו אותו והבינו מדעו להבדל לעמוד לפני ה' לשרתו ולעבדו לדעה את ה' והלך ישר כמו שעשהו האלקים הרי זה נתקדש קדש קדשים ויהיה ה' חלקו ונחלתו לעולם ולעולמי עולמים ויזכה לו בעה"ז.

Any individual in the world [earlier in the section he referred to Jews by name; here he is clearly speaking about all of humankind] whose spirit awakened them, whose wisdom guided them, to separate themselves, to stand before G-d, to serve G-d, to know G-d, and to grow in an upright fashion, just like G-d created them: such a person is sanctified as holy of holies. G-d will be his portion in the World to Come and in this world.

The Rambam quite clearly states that the highest level of spiritual greatness can be achieved by any man or women of any race and of any background. *Kol ish ve'ish*, anyone, can become *kodesh kodashim*, holy of holies.

This view is endorsed in the works of Rabbi Samson Raphael Hirsch, who, on numerous occasions when the Torah seems to discriminate against the inhabitants of Canaan, creatively interprets each section to be in line with the meritocracy that the Rambam promotes. No one is born into greatness. We must achieve it. And anyone and everyone is welcome to try.

According to the Rambam, a non-Jew can achieve the highest levels of spiritual superiority. This view is certainly not racist by any definition.

However, there is another view. In its extreme form, it is expressed by Rabbi Yehuda Halevi, author of a book known as the *Kuzari*. In section 1, he writes that the Jewish people possess what I will loosely translate as a spiritual gene, some intangible spiritual capacity that is passed from generation to generation. We have it, he writes, and non-Jews do not. And the fact that we have it sets us apart from all other nations. We are, according to this view, spiritually superior.[1]

This view is racist, at least according to the second definition that racism is the belief that different races have different qualities, especially a belief that deems one race superior to the next. This is it.

But what if we were to ask Rabbi Yehuda Halevi, what is the role of the Jewish people in the world? Why did G-d make us spiritually superior? To answer this question, he shares the following analogy: "The Jewish people are the heart of mankind" (*Kuzari* 1:43).

---

1   Rabbi Yehuda Halevi suggests that a convert cannot experience prophecy for this reason, as he or she is lacking this spiritual gene. The irony, of course, is that his book was written as a dialogue between a potential convert, the king of the Khazars, and a rabbi. It's worth noting that others who identify with this spiritual 'gene' understand that at conversion, the convert adopts a spiritual gene. This is mentioned explicitly by the Ohr Hachayyim and the Maharal.

Rabbi Yehuda Halevi, in describing the Jewish people as a heart, means to say that we are also connected to the other nations – the hands, the legs, the eyes. And in describing the Jewish people as a heart he means to say that we are here to *give* to the other nations.

So yes, Rabbi Yehuda Halevi believes that Jews are superior. But that is only in the sense that we are tasked with providing spiritual life to all the nations of the world. This is one of the most original sources that speak of the Jewish people's purpose as being a light unto the nations. While he does promote a theory that may be deemed as racistRabbi Yehuda Halevi also does not set forth a classic example of racism.[2]

So is Judaism racist? The answer is yes. At least according to one view promoted by many mystically-inclined scholars, and according to one definition of the term, Judaism does believe that Jews are a superior race. But where this theory differs from other racial theories is in *the implication of superiority*. Other racist groups that believe they are superior see the other group or groups as undeserving – underserving of land, undeserving of education, or, in the extreme, undeserving of life. But Rabbi Yehuda Halevi's view of superiority demands of the Jewish people to care more, to give more, and to be more, *especially* as it relates to others. We are the heart of the human race!

Moving to the question of skin color, are there biblical sources that indicate that certain colors are more beautiful than others? Once again, the answer is, it depends. Moshe's brother and sister describe Moshe's wife as being a Kushite, which means black. Commentators offer a wide variety of interpretations as to their intention. Rashi (Bamidbar 12:1) suggests that black is actually a euphemism for beauty. Others, such as Chizkiya ben Monoach, the Chizkuni (Bamidbar 12:1 s.v. *al*), understand that they were saying the exact opposite: the color of her skin made her *less* than attractive.

---

2   Ironically, the Rambam, in his introduction to *Perek Chelek* in *Maseches Sanhedrin*, explains that the world was created for the intellectually elite, and that the role of those who are not intellectually elite is to provide for the elite. While this is not a racist theory, it certainly is an extremely elitist one.

Is it appropriate to say that the cultural norms of the commentators' societies influenced their writings? I think so. To say that this latter commentator, writing in thirteenth-century France, had associated the color of one's skin with beauty based on the cultural norms of one's time tells us a lot about him. Even if we were to accept this racist approach as the only legitimate possibility, it still only informs us of the cultural norms of Moshe's time, and does not necessarily demonstrate that the Torah approves of this attitude. As an aside, even if the Torah was speaking negatively about black skin, the Torah was *not* endorsing white beauty. Caucasians simply did not exist in the Torah's time and place! If this entire shul would go back in time to the times of the Exodus, those who look like me, pale skin and all, would have a far harder time blending in with the Jewish people than those in this room who are black!

Either way, I don't see the Torah defining beauty for us as a universal norm. At most, this narrative is to be understood in context of the then-contemporary cultural norms.

So does Judaism promote a theory of race? Some say yes, and some say no. Are the Torah's laws that distinguish between one race and another predicated on a theory of superiority and inferiority? Some say yes and some say no. Does the Torah imply that the color of one's skin is associated with beauty or the lack thereof? Again, some say yes and others say no.

But now I want to share with you some things that are agreed upon by all commentators throughout time.

Is one permitted to speak negatively about an individual or a group of people? According to every Torah source, the answer is no. Unequivocally.

Is one allowed to make a person feel bad, inferior, or unwanted? According to every Torah source, the answer is no. Unequivocally.

Is one allowed to judge an individual or a group based on the color of their skin? Once again, according to every Torah source, the answer is no. Unequivocally.

I'm embarrassed that it has to be said, but it has to be said: there is no place for racial comments, for racial slurs (!), and for racial practices in Judaism. Yet I hear it all the time. Some of the comments are extreme and some are "benign," but all of it should be 100% unacceptable in our community. And it's not. *Let's be honest. You could make a racist joke among a group of Orthodox Jews and people will either laugh or, at the very least, you can get away with it.* That's unacceptable. I just don't get it. Even according to the most "racist" theory in Jewish thought, the idea is for us to care more, not less!

But let's get a little more personal and a little more practical. There is a crime issue in our community. Tuesday night there was a rash of violent crimes in the immediate area. In Cross Country, a man entered a home illegally and proceeded to tie the homeowner up so he could rob the house. A little while later, three men attacked two men on the street and took their belongings. The alleged perpetrators were all described as black.

Wednesday morning I was on my way to shul at approximately 6:00 a.m. It was dark outside. The streets were pretty empty. As I was heading to my car, I saw a tall black man and I froze.

I froze for almost a millisecond before I realized that it was my neighbor from down the block who was walking his dog. But you know what, and it hurts me to share this, but I know that he saw me freeze. He went out of his way to be as friendly as possible.

And so I ask you, as a community, how do we balance our legitimate security needs with the Torah's demand that we be kind, welcoming, and caring?

It goes without saying that racist slurs or putting down entire communities is not only counterproductive but is completely and patently against Jewish law. It is unequivocally forbidden to judge unfavorably, to speak negatively, or to make anyone feel put down in any way. So no, your concern when walking down the street is not *only* about when to take out your pepper spray or how quickly you should sprint across the street. Your concern when walking down the street must also be to try to say hello, to say good day, to make sure that you are fulfilling your role as a member of the Jewish faith, and maybe even the Jewish race, to look out and care for others.

As a community, our concern cannot only be about building walls and investing in better and better security. For every dollar we invest into Shomrim or NWCP (Northwest Citizens Patrol), should we not be investing at least half of that for programs that help rehabilitate the youth that are perpetrating these crimes? Should we not be joining hands with the black community in one way or another to bridge the tremendous divide that stands between us? Is that not a true reflection of Jewish values?

I hope you walk away from this talk with the following ideas. Yes, there is a strand of thought in normative Judaism that distinguishes between races. But even according to that view, the role of this so-called spiritual gene is not a license to be an arrogant or disparaging individual. It is an obligation to be a heart or a light to all people of all walks of life. According to all views, speaking negatively, making people feel uncomfortable, and even judging entire groups of people as one – all of that is blatantly against Jewish law.

I hope that after this talk, every time you think about protecting yourself, you also think about how you are caring for others, be it with a hello or by participating in or donating to the many organizations that are looking out for those who are less fortunate. They are our neighbors or, in the words of Rabbi Yehuda HaLevi, our hands or feet or eyes.

But I also hope you walk away with hope. Because despite all the negativity, I am filled with hope. Thank G-d, there have been many who have taken steps in the right direction. To name a few:

Former councilwoman Riki Spector was beaten a few years ago by two black teenagers. Today, she is an advocate for those same kids. She helped enroll them in U-Empower, one of many programs that empower youth in different underprivileged communities in Baltimore by giving them jobs and mentoring them while ensuring that they stay drug-free and in school.

A group from Shomrim recently started meeting with a black pastor from downtown to help work together on tackling crime, to share best practices and to create a bond.

And a synagogue in Pikesville decided to dedicate a Shabbos to having open and frank conversations about race, racism, and what it looks like for a Jewish community. (That would be us.)

So I am hopeful for a better tomorrow. Because it all starts with a conversation. Studies have shown that the way to break down walls between races is through dialogue, by getting to know one another. That's what we're doing today, and that's what I hope you continue to do tomorrow.

I'll conclude with a story. It inspires hope in me because I don't think it would have happened twenty or even ten years ago.

A little while ago, one of my children was trying to describe Tikvah Womack. My daughter said, "You know, she wears a cool scarf on her hair." I didn't know who she was talking about. A number of people wear scarves. "You know, she always smiles." A lot of people smile. "You know, she has a baby." Thank G-d, there are a lot of babies here. And finally she said, "You know, her skin is dark."

That was the fourth attempt she made at describing this person. Twenty years ago, ten years ago, I am confident that a child, and certainly a Jewish child, would have first said, "she is black." The child would have probably used a different word.[3] Thank G-d, we live in a day when that is no longer the case.

---

3   Rav Moshe Feinstein, the leading halakhic authority in America in the last century, in the midst of a complex responsa about the Jewish status of a group from Ethiopia, wrote the following: "And I suffered great anguish because I have heard that there are those in Israel who are not drawing them close in spiritual matters and are causing, G-d forbid, that they might be lost from Judaism. And it seems to me these people are behaving so only because the color of the Falashas' skin is black. It is obvious that one must draw them close, not only because they are no worse than the rest of the Jews [but also] because there is no distinction in practical application of the law because they are black…"

May we merit a day that "people will not be judged by the color of their skin, but by the content of their character." May we merit a day when the biblical and Jewish belief of *tzelem Elokim*, that *all of* mankind is created in G-d's image, is acknowledged and practiced by all.

Sermon Sponsored by
Pini, Adrienne and Natan Zimmerman

IN HONOR OF RABBI AND REBBETZIN MOTZEN ON TEN YEARS OF SERVICE TO the shul. Wishing you and NT another 10 years of success.

In memory of Adel & Kurt Maier, Bubby & Pop-Pop.

WHY KRUSTY THE CLOWN
ISN'T TORAH OBSERVANT

I'D LIKE TO SHARE WITH YOU AN ANALYSIS OF SEASON 3, EPISODE 6 OF THE Simpson's. My mother, G-d bless her, would lose her mind knowing that the show she was most appalled by in the 90s is the source of my sermon today. Ima, the show is still terrible, but the moral line of scrimmage has moved so far that The Simpson's is now the 2021 version of Leave it to Beaver.

The reason I'd like to discuss this episode of The Simpson's is because it is an excellent source-text for the many true roles of love in Judaism. (For those joining us as guests this morning, welcome to Ner Tamid, where we acknowledge that virtually everyone in this community has watched The Simpson's and try to make that meaningful! If you'd like to walk out, now is a perfect time…)

Here's a synopsis: There's this guy called Krusty the Clown. He's depressed, he's antisocial, he's an addict. He hates himself yet the children love him. Krusty the Clown is an outsized reminder of something we all know – that fame and adoration do not, on their own, bring joy.

Where does his depression stem from? The show's writers never make it clear. But in season 3, episode 6, we learn about his childhood. It turns out that Krusty is Jewish. Not only is he Jewish, but his father was a rabbi, and his father was a rabbi, and his father… you get the point. The story goes that Krusty's father, Rabbi Hyman Krustofsky, who is played by none other than Jackie Mason, wanted his son to be a rabbi, but Krusty was not interested. Krusty wanted to go into show business. And yet he didn't want to hurt his father. Eventually he did go into comedy, his father found out, and he banished his son from his life, wanting nothing to do with him.

Now I'm going to pause because there's a certain symmetry here. As many of you know, Jackie Mason was born Yakov Moshe Hakohen Maza.

His father was considered by some to be on par with another fellow Lower East Sider – HaRav Moshe Feinstein. Jackie Mason came from a long line of esteemed rabbis and his father desperately wanted his son to become a rabbi. I've always wondered how Jackie Mason felt taking on this role of Rabbi Krustofsky, giving voice to what were likely very similar conversations his father had with him.

And it begs a question every parent must face. We all have dreams for our children. We all want them to be healthy, to not inherit our flaws, only our best qualities, to succeed in life, and to be contributing members of society and good Jews. In an earlier generation, parents could tell their children what to do; they could make demands of their children. But sometimes it went too far, especially as it pertained to religion. In a flashback scene from that episode, we find Krusty's father strangling him when he implied that he's not interested in Judaism. There are many Krustys have who felt strangled, not literally but figuratively. Collectively, as a Jewish people, we realized that the fire and brimstone approach was the wrong one or is at least, no longer relevant, so the words "love" and "joy" were rediscovered and brought into our spiritual lexicon.

But unfortunately, the pendulum has swung too far. Whereas in the past parents were too strict, now they're too lenient. Whereas in the past parents would not think twice before correcting their children's every mistake, they now are afraid to give their children any direction. And there are terrible consequences. Children crave structure. Children need structure. Rules are crucial to the development of self-discipline. Rules and structure are the greatest gifts a parent can give their child. These are gifts they may not appreciate today, but they will regret not having them in the future.

To be clear, this is not a Jewish problem; it's a societal problem. But as Jews, it gets a little more complicated. I hear from parents who don't want to push their children too much so they "pick their battles." They will push their children to study and to get them tutors and to find support until they get straight A's in math and science, etc. But when it comes to Jewish practices or Jewish studies they say, "I don't want to be too strict." Or my favorite, "I want my children to discover the beauty of Judaism on their own." I've never heard anyone say, "I want my children to discover the beauty of math and English on their own. If they want to go to school, it's their choice." If it's real to you, if you believe that the Torah is a way of life, that G-d is real and we Jews have a special role to play, this ain't the place to let the children decide.

So how do we find that balance? The balance between not strangling the child and not being afraid to discipline her? Between the seriousness of our calling as Jews and the joys of having a relationship with our Creator?

I am really not sure. I don't have a formula – I wish I did. What I do know is that each and every parent must seriously grapple with this question of how we calibrate strictness with compassion, our vision of who our children should be with who they want to become, our respect for their choices and the conviction of our own.

Should we get back to The Simpson's?

Bart and Lisa learn that Krusty is estranged from Rabbi Krustofsky, and they devise a plan to reconcile father and son. Lisa does some research and sends Bart to go persuade Rabbi Krustofsky. And the two of them, Bart and Rabbi Krustofsky, take part in a debate of sorts. Bart says, "Rabbi, does it not say in the Talmud that you should bring close with the right hand and push away with the left?" To which the rabbi responds, "Yes, but it also says, Honor one's mother and father." Bart says, "The Torah says that one should be soft like a reed and not stiff like a cedar." To which the rabbi responds, "Yes, but it also says, You should study the Torah day and night."

It's an amazing dialogue and one, to the credit of the writers of The Simpson's, that was well-researched, unlike too many other modern shows that depict Orthodox Jews. Maybe I'm reading too deeply into this, but there's much more than a fight over biblical teachings taking place between Bart and Rabbi Krustofsky. Bart is speaking to the meta of Judaism, some of the big ideas: compassion, flexibility, and change. Rabbi Krustofsky is speaking to particular *mitzvos: kabed es avicha ve'es imecha*, and the mitzvah of studying Torah.

There is a constant tension in Judaism between the forest and the trees. There are denominations within Judaism that only focus on the forest, the big ideas of Judaism, like justice or being a light unto the nations. They ignore the trees, like Shabbos, kosher, and *taharas hamishpacha*. There are other denominations that do the opposite: they study Torah, they keep all the *mitzvos* to a T, but there are no guiding principles. They live a spiritually myopic life, not caring about the larger role they have been asked to play in the world.

The Torah portion we read today begins and ends with the details of the Torah, most famously, *"Vehaya im shomo'a tishme'u el mitzvosai,"* "If you keep my commandments." G-d lays out the "tree" version of the Torah: do what's right and you get rewarded, do what's wrong and you get punished. It's a small-minded vision. But then in the center of the parsha, Moshe poetically calls out, *"Ma Hashem elokecha sho'el me'imach,"* "What does G-d really want?" What's the big picture? What's this *really* all about? *"Leyir'a es Hashem,"* "to be in awe of G-d," *"ule'ahava oso,"* "and to love Him."

You see, Rabbi Krustofsky and Bart were both right. Judaism, like any relationship, is made up of tremendous and powerful feelings expressed in small and seemingly insignificant ways. All relationships are fueled by a vision of deep and passionate love. But it's generated by small gestures: by putting our phone down and making eye contact, by filling up a tank of gas and taking out the garbage, by allowing yourself to lose an argument and by giving a word of encouragement. Our relationship with G-d, no different than our relationship with other humans, has a big picture and many small details that bring the picture into focus.

Now the Rambam has a different take on the contradiction between the small-minded vision of the Torah, including *mitzvos* and *aveiros* as well as reward and punishment, and the big picture of love. In his commentary on the Mishnah, he suggests that there are stages and levels in our relationship with G-d. When we are young and immature, our relationship with G-d is one of details, instructions, and reward and punishment. I'll do what's right and get a mitzvah note from G-d. That's who the section of *Vehaya im shomo'a* is addressing. But as we progress, mature, and become spiritually sophisticated, our connection to G-d becomes so much more than this mitzvah or that mitzvah. It blossoms, or is meant to blossom, into a relationship of respect, awe, and love.

What the Rambam is speaking to is that in every relationship, there are levels. People say they fell in love with someone. Cool. That's great. Guess what? You can fall in love with the same person again. And again. And again.

If you constantly invest in your relationship, the depth and the passion are endless. If you're constantly looking to find new ways to give, if you're open to the fact that you never really know your significant other and you approach them with a constant state of curiosity, you will fall in love over and over and over again.

In the final scene of that Simpson's episode, Krusty the Clown reconciles with his father. There's no conversation between them, no explanation. They see each other with tears in their eyes and they embrace. For an episode with so much depth, I was hoping for more dialogue, for them to spend a little more time discussing their differences until they could properly reconcile. Is it really accurate that father and son see each other after all these years and just embrace in love?

Dr. Erich Fromm, in his wonderfully insightful book *The Art of Loving*, suggests that love does not come naturally to us. But the Sefas Emes in this week's parsha disagrees. Addressing the question of how the Torah can mandate us to love our fellow Jew and how the Torah can mandate us to love Hashem, the Sefas Emes writes that love is innate. There is a *nekuda*, a dot, a spark of love, that exists within each and every one of us: a love for children, a love for a spouse, a love for everyone, and ultimately a love for G-d. That spark of love is waiting to explode, to burst out, to find expression. Yes, a father and son who have been estranged for years can see each other, and their love can find true expression immediately.

One final story, which brings us back to where we began: the overlapping stories of Krusty the Clown and Jackie Mason. In what was likely the final interview with the famous comedian, Rabbi Moshe Taub, a rabbi and historian, met up with Jackie Mason and his wife to talk about growing up on the Lower East Side. In the process of the interview, they got talking about Jackie Mason's relationship with Rav Moshe Feinstein. Mason received his *semicha* from the famed rabbi, and the interviewer was curious about their relationship, especially after Jackie Mason dropped out of the rabbinate and eventually stopped observing Jewish Law. Taub was shocked to learn that Jackie Mason and Rav Moshe continued to meet through all the years.

Unable to contain himself, the rabbi asked the comedian, "What did Rav Moshe say to you in those meetings?" In other words, how did Rav Moshe respond to this former student who had walked away from the rabbinate and observant religion as we know it?

Jackie Mason looked Rabbi Taub in the eyes and told him: There was only one message he conveyed to me in every one of our conversations: love, love, love.

While this story is both beautiful and shocking, it really should not be. In today's Haftara, we read how the Jewish people, after having committed horrendous sins, assumed that G-d had forsaken them. How could G-d have anything to do with such sinners? Why would He want to stay in touch in any way?

Hashem lovingly responds, "Does a mother forget her child?" (Yeshayahu 49:15). Of course I will never forsake you. You are my child and I love you.

Love gets a bad rap in Judaism. Ask an academic and they'll tell you that love is a Christian trait. Ask some of the most observant Jews and they will poo-poo love. They'll argue for *yiras shamayim*, the fear and dread of Heaven, but love, they'll tell you, is fluff.

And it's just not true. Love is paramount in Judaism. Love is the core emotion in Judaism: a love for one another, a love for oneself, and a love for Hashem.

Yes, as we discussed, it needs calibration. And at the same time, if done right, we can fall deeper and deeper in love, falling for our loved ones and for G-d time and time again.

The prayer that every parent must have for their children is that they appreciate the central role of love in Judaism – and not just for our children. May we all recognize that we have the capacity *to be loved and to love*. May we all learn to appreciate the value of the trees and the value of the forest, never losing sight of one for the other. And may we all experience the incredible joy of falling in love over and over and over again.

Section IV:

A VISION FOR
A SYNAGOGUE

I HAVE A DREAM FOR OUR SHUL

Sometimes – quite often, actually – I am asked a version of the following question: "Rabbi, what's your dream for Ner Tamid?"

Typically these questions are a cover for a very particular question. Though people use broad words like "vision" or "dream," they're really just trying to avoid using a word that rhymes with pizza. Or maybe *metzitza*. And like pizza and *metzitza*, it's a topic that is controversial and gives many people indigestion (*mechitza*).

But today, it's the last Shabbos of this crazy pandemic year, so I will answer the question. Are you ready?

This is my vision, my dream for Ner Tamid:

This past week, someone joined us for evening services. He was in mourning and asked to lead davening. He also happened to be a Satmar chosid, and so his davening sounded something like this:*"Boo-reech ahtaw…"* I loved it because *I dream of a shul in which Jews of all stripes feel comfortable in these walls. All Jews. And that means that on Shabbos, no one should be able to find parking for at least five blocks around the shul, not because we endorse driving to shul on Shabbos but because people who do drive feel comfortable coming to our shul. It means that in the shul, you will see streimels and T-shirts, black hats and doilies, kippot serugot and no covering at all. All Jews. A shul in which Jews of all races, orientations, and identifications can say, "This place is my spiritual home."*

Though we sometimes struggle with our weekday minyan, what I love about it is its intimacy. It is such a small crowd that everyone seems to know each other's name, everyone knows when a regular is missing. *I dream of a shul where we may not all be best friends – that's not realistic – but where everyone knows everyone's name. A shul in which, if someone is missing even for a Shabbos, they get a call or a text to let them know they were missed.*

Many children in this shul went to camp this summer. I love sleepaway camp. The energy that is generated in those settings is very hard to replicate anywhere else. In speaking to these boys and girls there is one recurring theme: regardless of where they went to camp, one of their top highlights is Friday night services in camp, in which the campers, counselors, and head staff would welcome Shabbos with beautiful energy-filled singing and dancing. The energy in summer camps is awesome. *I dream of a shul in which every Shabbos tefilla is like camp. A shul in which no one feels any inhibitions and lets loose with full-throated singing, with spirited dancing, every time the siddur opens.*

Someone who is part of our community told me he's going to Uman this Rosh Hashana. Every year there is a mass pilgrimage of Jews who go to the site of Rav Nachman of Breslov's grave and celebrate Rosh Hashana there. These men leave their wives back at home – it's men only. Someone sent me a meme in which a man tells his wife he's going to Uman for Rosh Hashana and she says, "No problem. When you're at the holy site, do yourself a favor and pray for a good *shidduch.*"

These people go to Uman because they can't find services that are so soulful in America. *I dream of a shul in which these spiritual seekers can find comfort. A shul that is pin-drop quiet, but not deathly quiet – those shuls in which you're afraid to talk lest you get silenced by the shushing czar. A shul in which people are quiet the way they are quiet in a museum of fine art: they are so moved that they just cannot speak.*

One of our members, Nomi Maine, celebrated her Bat Mitzvah this weekend. When Nomi and I were talking this past week, I learned that she is a big fan of Ariana Grande, a very popular singer. She told me that she wouldn't mind getting a bottle of Ariana Grande's latest perfume. I didn't buy her a bottle of perfume as a gift, but I did look it up, and it turns out that her latest perfume is called "G-d is a Woman," and it's inspired by Ariana's song by the same name. I looked up the lyrics of the song – and I quickly decided to not talk about the song!

However, the subtext of the song's title is a powerful challenge – why is G-d always referred to as a man? Why not a woman? Within the English language, it's a good question; why do we 'genderfy' Hashem? In Hebrew, of course, everything, even inanimate objects, is either masculine or feminine, so you have to pick one. But the challenge is not really about G-d; it's about power; it's about inequality; it's about roles. And these are tough topics in society and especially for Torah-observing Jews. We do believe that there are different roles for men and women as expressed through the different *mitzvos*. We also recognize that as opposed to a family setting, where there is spiritual equality, or, if anything, a far stronger set of responsibilities and opportunities for women, in a *shul* setting, which has particular emphasis on minyan and things of that nature, Judaism comes across as terribly skewed.

I dream of a shul in which we do not oversimplify, in which we do not just do what others are doing, in which we continue to grapple with this question, and yet we create endless opportunities for growth, spiritual experiences, and advanced learning for women.

One thing that I love about our shul is that people care so deeply about communal and global issues. It is a community with a big heart. *I dream of a shul in which that heart is expressed in action, in doing, in taking on projects, in using our collective energy to not just talk about the world around us but to change it.*

We are a shul of Zionists and, every once in a while, families get up and move to Israel. Making *aliyya* is not for everyone. *But I dream of a shul in which we are constantly losing members because they are moving to Eretz Yisroel. These members are replaced by new members. And then we continue to lose members to aliyya, who are replaced by new members. And on and on.*

I dream of a shul in which Torah learning plays a central role in everyone's life. In which classes are a supplement but everyone, in their own way, has a unique and personal relationship with our unbelievable heritage and spends time every day, at home or at shul, studying these sacred texts, growing through the uplifting teachings of our Sages.

*I dream of a shul in which we comfortably talk about G-d and comfortably talk **to** G-d.*

Lastly, one of the most famous and moving messages of the prophets are the words of Malachi: "*Hinei Anochi sholei'ach lachem es Eliyahu hanavi*" *(3:23)*. G-d promises the Jewish people that one day in the future, He will send Elijah the prophet to herald the messianic era. Malachi continues, "*Veheishiv lev avos al banim*," "and the hearts of parents will return through the hearts of their children." *This is the ultimate Jewish dream, for our children to surpass us spiritually. This is the messianic vision of Malachi, that the arc of the spiritual universe is long, but it bends further with each generation.*

And that is my dream for all the children and really all the members of our shul. That they live this dream. That they experience what it is to be a member of a community, of a shul in which everyone is accepted, in which the prayers are soulful and services are magically silent, in which people are constantly dancing and singing in prayer, in which girls and women, and boys and men, find opportunity, endless opportunity for spiritual growth, in which we change the face of our community by rolling up our sleeves, in which we deepen our connection to the land of Israel, in which we are all well-versed in Torah, Gemara, Halacha, and Jewish thought, in which we all have a relationship with G-d. I dream that the children not only experience this reality but that they pave the way to make it happen. That is my dream.

There is a famous question: why do we first celebrate Rosh Hashana and then Yom Kippur? Shouldn't we first atone for our sins and then clean ourselves of our misdeeds, starting the year with a fresh slate? It seems out of order.

Our Sages explain that the goal of Rosh Hashana is to think about the dream, the big picture, where we really want to be. Once we crystallize that picture, we then zoom in and focus on the many things that are getting in the way. And so we first celebrate Rosh Hashana, when we accept G-d's kingship and our role in His world. And then on Yom Kippur we focus on our sins, the many impediments that are preventing us from living up to that dream.

There are details that we, as a shul, need to address if we want to live this dream. But they are details. Let's not lose sight of the big picture. Let's not lose sight of the dream.

May we be done with all the trials and tribulations of these past two years. May G-d bless us with peace, harmony, and health, so that we, together, can transform all our dreams into reality.

DEDICATIONS

If Ner Tamid was a shul that masked during Covid....Dayeinu.

If Ner Tamid was a shul that masked during Covid and also had a rabbi whose speeches and classes were engaging and meaningful...Dayeinu.

If Ner Tamid was a shul that masked during Covid, had a rabbi whose speeches and classes were engaging and meaningful and was a place where all feel comfortable...Dayeinu.

If Ner Tamid was a shul that masked during Covid, had a rabbi whose speeches and classes were engaging and meaningful, was a place where everyone feels comfortable, with a Rabbi and Rebbetzin who go out of their way to know each of us personally....Dayeinu.

If Ner Tamid was a shul that masked during Covid, had a rabbi whose speeches and classes were engaging and meaningful, was a place where everyone feels comfortable, with a Rabbi and Rebbetzin who go out of their way to know each of us personally, where a wide range of people with different backgrounds and experiences grow together...Dayeinu.

With much appreciation to Rabbi and Mrs. Motzen as well as Adina B. who put so much into making the shul an inspiring and welcoming place.

Tzvi and Batsheva Atlas

Rabbi Yisrael and Rebbetzin Hindy Motzen,

Mazel Tov on this milestone.

May you continue to be the "someone
for everyone."

May Hashem grant you continued success
and bracha in the work you do.

Sherri and Gary Bauman

Keep up the great work you are doing for our shul and the Baltimore community. We are so appreciative of all your efforts.

Jay and Dina Bernstein

In honor of Rabbi and Rebbetzin Motzen and with tremendous thanks for their compassion, kindness, and generosity.

Matthew and Dara Bernstein

Mazel Tov to Rabbi and Hindy Motzen on ten
fabulous years of dedication and inspiration.

Shirley and Howard Blumenfeld

Mazal tov on 10 years!

Thank you for your Torah wisdom
and kindness.

May your inspiration continue to reach so
many, near and far.

Simon and Tara Cornberg

In honor of Rabbi and Mrs. Motzen on their tenth anniversary at Ner Tamid.

Deborah Dopkin

Shushi and Yona Ehrenfeld

Mazel Tov to Rabbi and Rebbetzin Motzen
on ten years at Ner Tamid. Thank you for all
that you do for our community.

Heather and Evan Fisher

The 70-year history of five generations of our family have been blessed by having Ner Tamid as our shul. My uncle, Harold W. Siegel was a founding member of the then, Greenspring Valley Synagogue. When my family moved two blocks away from the shul, it became an important part of our family life.

My grandmother, who lived with us, was in shul every Shabbos. My parents were involved in almost every facet of Shul life, from service on the Board, to president of the Sisterhood and PTA, to man of the year of the Brotherhood.

Our children both graduated from the Hebrew School and celebrated their bar and bat mitzvahs at our Shul. One of our granddaughters, Lauren, and her fiancée, were both fortunate to have Rabbi Motzen as their Rabbinics teacher when they were in high school. To this day, our daughter, granddaughters and I sit in the same seats that my grandmother, mother and I have sat in for over six decades.

Our family has been blessed with three wonderful rabbis, who we have had the honor of knowing at Ner Tamid. Rabbi Motzen and Hindy have truly been an inspiration to our family. Their warmth, knowledge and commitment to every member of our Shul have been extraordinary. Their involvement, not just at Ner Tamid, but throughout our community at large, demonstrates their commitment to enriching Jews and non-Jews. They clearly serve as our shul's ambassadors, and we are all proud of what they have accomplished and will accomplish in the years to come.

Mazel Tov and all our Best Wishes on this momentous occasion,

Susan and Howard Goldberg

Thank you, Rabbi and Rebbetzin Motzen for helping us through the twists and turns of our lives. We are so grateful that you are on this journey with us.

Mazel tov on this wonderful milestone, to another 10 years and beyond.

Sam, Yael, Gabby, and
(your #1 fan) Ariel Goldstein

Congratulations on ten years of showering us with your guidance, knowledge, and leadership. You are a towering source of inspiration. May HaShem continue to support you, as you support us, and may you, Hindy, and your family continue to find nachas and blessing from us.

Janet Hankin

Congratulations to the Motzens on completing the first decade of your service to Ner Tamid.

Stanley and Elissa Hellman

Dear Rabbi and Rebbetzin Motzen,

Mazal Tov on this momentous occasion. We are in awe of all you do for this community, and we thank you for all of your support.

We look forward too many more years of your leadership.

Julie and Jacob Karasik

Thanks to Rabbi and Rebbetzin Motzen
for your long-time friendship and
support. Congratulations on your ten
year anniversary. You both have infused a
tremendous amount of Yiddishkeit and love
into our Shul and the great Baltimore area as
a whole. We wish you many more simchas,
and a continued life filled with Torah.

Mazel Tov,

Marina, Adam, Sophia and Jordan Klaff

We have seen and experienced much over our many years in Baltimore.

Rabbi and Rebbetzin Motzen are a major force in Ner Tamid and the community. They are unique, warm, real, with no agendas, and treat everyone with same kovod. They simply practice what they preach. Just wonderful leaders.

We couldn't be happier on your 10th anniversary at Ner Tamid.

Mazal Tov! May you go from Strength to Strength.

Adriane and Harry Kozlovsky

Thank you, Rabbi and Rebbetzin Motzen for making Ner Tamid such a warm and welcoming place. The two of you seem to have boundless energy. It's good you started young…

Naomi and Mike Kraut

With much
Appreciation and Gratitude
to
Rabbi and Rebbetzin Hindy Motzen
for their
Exemplary devotion and commitment
to being
outstanding
Spiritual Leaders
for
Ner Tamid's congregants
and
Am Yisrael.

Zev Lewis
The M.B. Lewis Charitable Foundation

Rabbi and Rebbetzin Motzen,

- Thank you for challenging us.
- Thank you for inspiring us.
- Thank you for loving us.

We are so blessed to be part of the Ner Tamid community under your leadership. We can't wait for the next 10 years!!!

Sheryl, Avi, Meira, Ben, Simcha and Natanel Lopin

Mazel Tov to Ner Tamid and Rabbi and Rebbetzin Motzen.

Dr. and Mrs. Lucas

With appreciation to Rabbi and Rebbetzin
Motzen on both a personal and communal
level for your inspiration, care and leadership.

Lisa and Aron Martin

You two are absolutely amazing! Thank you! Thank you! Thank you!

Cerrill Meister

For the first time in my life, I belong to a shul where I am accepted just as I am and where I am inspired to be the best version of myself.

Thank you, Rabbi and Rebbetzin Motzen for being such a positive force in our community - I am so grateful to you both.

In honor of the most amazing congregation,
Ner Tamid.

Rabbi Yisrael and Hindy Motzen

To Rabbi and Rebbetzin Motzen,

Thank you for all of your devotion and hard work for Ner Tamid and the community at large.

Sincerely, Mike, Ora, Ami, Lila, and Aaron Noorani

Mazel Tov Rabbi and Rebbetzin Motzen in honor of your 10 years of dedicated service to Ner Tamid Congregation and the Jewish Community.

You visit the sick and comfort members in times of loss; always reaching out to those in need. Your kindness shows no boundaries.

You are both exemplary role models for the entire Jewish Community. You make Purim and Pesach fun, Rosh Hashana and Yom Kippur meaningful, and all the holidays filled with holiness. We feel blessed to have you both as our Rabbi and Rebbetzin.

As two stars among the great lights, may your brightness continue to shine for decades to come. May Hashem continue to bless you and your family.

Rhona and Stan Plunka and Family

My family and I wish you a warm, hearty mazel tov on your 10th anniversary as Rabbi at Ner Tamid. Thanks for all you have done and will continue to do to keep Ner Tamid relevant and enriched. May you continue to successfully lead Ner Tamid for many years to come. Yasher Koach!

The Scherr, Colker and Ezrine Families

To Rabbi and Rebbetzin Motzen,

You are both an inspiration to all of us at Ner Tamid. Please accept our most heartfelt Mazel Tov, and our deepest gratitude for the incredible work you do.

With love, gratitude, and admiration,

Raymond Rosenblatt

With so much gratitude to the Rabbi and Rebbetzin from the bottom of my heart.

Esther Rosenbloom

Kol Ha Kavod! May you both be granted the strength, patience, insight, and rachamim to continue to share your gifts with the congregation and the community to help us embrace and be engaged by the light and wisdom of Torah that we may each become better people and more engaged Jews.

David and Shelly Schwartz

Rabbi and Rebbetzin Motzen,

Congratulations on your 10-year Anniversary. You both are and may you continue to be, Shining Stars for Ner Tamid and our Community.

Karen and Mark Schwartzman

Thank you for all you do!

Anonymous

In honor of a Rabbi and Rebbetzin that are paradigms of leadership, sensitivity, thoughtfulness and caring for those around them. Wishing them many more years of good health and continued success in their work on behalf of Klal Yisrael.

Zevy and Sara Wolman and Family

Ten years ago, we started our journey into Orthodox Judaism. It started with walking into Ner Tamid for Kabbalas Shabbos, we were nervous and full of trepidation at the social anxiety of being in a new environment. How will they accept us? What we found was a loving Rabbi and Rebbetzin that have always supported us from day one. That first night Rabbi and Rebbetzin opened their homes and their hearts, that's just what they do. Over the last 10 years they have been there for our family in every way possible, both in times of pain and in times of joy. There is no way to truly thank them for how they have shown up for us in our lives. People ask us all the time what's our story. The truth is we are unsure there would even be a story without the Motzens. One time a tragedy happened to our family. Rabbi Motzen called us, and we were distraught. He listened, we told him how disappointed we were with the situation, and he replied that he was humbled. Based on the tragedy it was a response we were not expecting from a spiritual leader. We expected a speech, a story about how we should be strong or keep the faith, but no it was the sincerity of his humanness that allowed us to move through that moment. The Motzens truly have special neshamas and most importantly it is their humility that makes them such giants in our eyes. We used to joke with the Rabbi that he has a main line to Hashem because his drashas always seemed to speak to the moment of what we and others were going through. Truth is, it's because he has a main line to his people, he really listens. If he has an answer he'll give it, but if he doesn't, he won't, which is rare and admirable in a leader. We are beyond blessed to celebrate this milestone with them. Rabbi and Rebbetzin Motzen may our families journey together in the next ten years, joys outweighing the pains from strength to strength.

Love,

Tikvah, Tzadik, Yishai, Yisrael, and Yaaziel Womack

Your impact is
immeasurable.
Thank you!

*Chavi and
Moshe Abramson*

Ten years to the power
of two.

May we keep both
of you for a hundred
and twenty.

Ken and Sue Besser

Thank you to Rabbi
and Rebbetzin Motzen
for all your do for
the Ner Tamid and
Baltimore community.
May you merit to
continue your sacred
work for many,
many years.

*Ezra and
Ariella Bernstein*

Mazel Tov Rabbi and
Rebbetzin Motzen!

*Drs. Debra and
Howard Birenbaum*

In honor of Rabbi and Rebbetzin Motzen for all they do!

*Zvi and
Miriam Birnbaum*

In honor of the whole Motzen family! So grateful to be part of the Ner Tamid family!

Adina Burstyn

Your presence has been a needed positive addition to our community as a whole and to us as individuals. Here's to the next 10 years!

*Jill and
Bruce Blumenthal*

With much gratitude and appreciation for Rabbi and Rebbetzin Motzen for making Ner Tamid a spiritual and communal home for our family. Thank you for the inspiration, warmth, wisdom, and dedication.

*Sincerely, Aaron, Nilly,
Miriam and Elan Ciner*

Congratulations
Rabbi for 10 years
of outstanding
service at Ner Tamid
and our wonderful
Jewish community.

*Larry Chernikoff and
Ken Coleman*

One of my most exciting
accomplishments as
Congregation President was
sharing the Bima with you on
your first Shabbos as the 3rd
Rabbi in our shul's history! It's
been an incredible 10 years!
Wishing my Rabbi, my
wonderful friends, Rabbi &
Hindy Motzen, everything
good as they continue to lead
our Ner Tamid family with
love!!
Phil Cohen & Family

Thank you & kudos
dear Motzens on this
decade of growth
milestone. Your words
and actions are always
inspirational. Gratitude
to Dad z'l and Mom
for instilling loyalty
to our beloved Ner
Tamid family- Past,
Present, Future.

*Love, D of PDB
& Cohens*

Thank you Rabbi and
Rebbetzin Motzen
for always inspiring
us on a weekly basis
with your uplifting
words and thoughts. So
much of what you say
enhances our daily life.

With
sincere appreciation,

*Chaya and
Leibel Cooper*

Congratulations
on your 10-year
anniversary serving
Ner Tamid. May you
have another successful
10 years!

Gudrun Dunn

Rabbi and Rebbetzin Motzen
continue to amaze us with
their generosity, kindness,
and willingness to help
anyone that crosses their
path. They are two of the
most giving people that we
have ever met. We feel blessed
to have them in our loves.
Mazel tov on celebrating 10
years and we look forward to
the next 10!

Yaakov and Sho Englander

In honor of Rabbi
and Mrs. Motzen,
whose leadership
adds so much to our
community. May
they continue their
wonderful work on
behalf of Klal Yisrael
for many years
to come.

*Linda and
Michael Elman*

Mazel Tov to Rabbi
and Rebbetzin Motzen
on ten years of
service to Ner Tamid!
Thank you for your
leadership and love to
the congregation and
the community.

Neil Frater

With much gratitude to Rabbi and Rebbetzin Motzen for all that you do for our shul. May we continue to share davening, learning and simcha in the years to come. We wish you hatzlacha raba in all that you do!

Lisa and Murray Friedman

Mazel Tov to the Motzens on their 10-year anniversary with Ner Tamid!

Steve Goloskov

וּקְנֵה לְךָ חָבֵר, וֶהֱוֵי דָן אֶת כָּל הָאָדָם לְכַף זְכוּת" "עֲשֵׂה לְךָ רַב,

פרקי אבות א: ו

"Accept a teacher upon yourself, acquire a friend and judge everyone favorably." Ethics of the Fathers, 1:6. This pasuk describes Rabbi and Rebbetzin Motzen perfectly! Thank you for your teachings, friendship, guidance, support and tireless efforts on behalf of our shul and community. May Hashem continue to bless you and your beautiful family.

Arnie and Nina Allen-Goldberg

We are ever grateful to have found such a spiritual leader possessing:

- an open heart and an open mind
- deep traditional learning and insights into contemporary culture
- an enthusiastic teacher and an empathetic listener

ופעל צדק ודבר אמת בלבבו. הולך תמים

Jonathan and Rachel Groner

With tremendous hakarat hatov to the Motzen Family and Ner Tamid for being my family here in Baltimore and a life raft during the storms.

With hakarat hatov to Ner Tamid and PARTICULARLY to NT Montessori.

Yael Henry

Thanks for a memorable 10 Years. We look forward to the next 10!

Harriet & Elliot Jacob

To Rabbi and Rebbetzin Motzen,

Kol hakavod for all you have done for our family and for so many others in the entire community. May you continue to grow and to go from strength to strength.

Bill Heyman and Family

Mazel Tov Rabbi and Mrs. Motzen. You are very caring, bright, compassionate, and inclusive. During your leadership these ten years, Ner Tamid has flourished greatly.

Baila and Murray Jacobson

With tremendous hakarat hatov to the Motzen Family and Ner Tamid for being my family here in Baltimore and a life raft during the storms.

With hakarat hatov to Ner Tamid and PARTICULARLY to NT Montessori.

Yael Henry

Rabbi and Rebbetzin Motzen: It is with tremendous gratitude that we thank you for leading our shul and community for 10 years. As Neil Young, a fellow landsman, sang on his own Decade: "long may you run."

Michael and Aviva Kidorf

Mazel tov to Rabbi and Rebbetzin Motzen for being the community pillars they are.

In honor of our wonderful daughter, Adina Meister.

Shout out to our family Deborah H. and Adina B. who contribute so much to Ner Tamid.

Shalom and Syma Kelman

No matter how eloquent the speeches were or how strong the hugs have been or how sincerely felt the words placed in the book were & are, there's really no way to FULLY express the depth of our appreciation, respect, & love that we, ourselves, & all in the Ner Tamid family feel for the 2 of you. חיל אל מחיל!

Thank you! Thank you!

Michael and Barbara Klaff

To the Rabbi and Rebbetzin: Thank you so very much for your wonderful and inspiring work. Mazal Tov on reaching this milestone!

Martin and Margie Koretzky

Thank you to Rabbi and Rebbetzin for your unparalleled guidance! Hatzlacha!

Ruby and Simon Lasker

In 10 years of leadership, Rabbi and Rebbetzin Motzen have taken the shul which has always been my home and built something that is both comfortingly familiar and refreshingly revolutionary. I am grateful for their leadership and for the beautiful community which they have built.

Sara Kuperman

Rabbi and Rebbetzin,

Thank you for staying another 10 years.

Ella and Jesse Levy

Rabbi Motzen and Hindy,

You are a perfect example of a marriage made in heaven. The work you and Hindy do for the shul is uplifting. The sermons on Shabbat, the shiurs on Thursday and the Tehillim group once and month are so special. I feel honored to have you as my Rabbi and Rebbetzin. We are so blessed to have you as special leaders of our shul, Ner Tamid.

Good health, happiness and a long life to you and your family.

Estelle Levitas

Thoughtful.
Courageous.
Scholarly.
Empathetic. Wise.
Curious. Serious.
Funny. Inspiring.
Creative.
Dedicated.
Spiritual.
Thank you.

*Barry and
Shelley List*

Congratulations on your 10 years of inspiring, teaching, and caring service to Ner Tamid and far beyond.

Dr. Noah and Ellen Lightman

With great appreciation to Rabbi Motzen and all the wonderful lay leaders of Ner Tamid!

*Aaron and
Aliza Loeb*

With great respect
and admiration.

*Jeffery and Shira
London and Family*

About 2 years ago, I attended
a presentation of Rabbi
Motzen and knew I had
found the right religious
home for me. I live in
Annapolis but enjoy every
Shabbos at Ner Tamid.
Mazel Tov to the Rabbi and
Rebbetzin Motzen and all
the wonderful members of
Ner Tamid.

Susan Millman

Mazel Tov to Rabbi
and Rebbetzin Motzen
on their special
10th anniversary
with Ner Tamid and
wishing them many
more years together
with their warm and
growing Kehila.

*Layne and
Mike Lowenstein*

Mazel Tov and
thank you Rabbi and
Rebbetzin Motzen.

*From the
Mordfin Family*

Kol hakavod to my dear son and daughter in law, Rabbi Yisrael and Hindy Motzen.

Abba and Marsha

Thank you for your inspiration and all you do. You are very unique and special people. We are lucky to have both of you.

Susan and Monroe Musman

To my dear children; Rabbi Sruli and Hindy,

Mazal tov on reaching this milestone of 10 years of service to Ner Tamid. I admire the myriad of innovations you've contributed to your shul and your dedication, enthusiasm, and effort you exert behind the scenes.

Best of all, whenever I introduce myself in Baltimore, I am asked if I am related to you. Many people told me that they joined the shul because of your warmth and inclusiveness.

I am proud and grateful to be your mother.

May Hashem bless you and your children with good health, fulfillment, and nachas from one another.

Love,
Ima Motzen

Mazel Tov! We are blessed to have you in our lives. Your kindness, caring and inspiring words meant so much to Harry z"l, as they do me. May Hashem bless you with many years at Ner Tamid!

Sonia Ostrow

על שלשה דברים העולם עומד

Rabbi and Rebbetzin: we thank you for being a shining example and creating a shul that all three are of great importance: תורה, עבודה, גמילות חסדים

We appreciate the friendship, the guidance and the love we feel when we spend time at our second home. With much gratitude and respect.

Jonathan, CG, Yonina, and Kayla Polirer

We love the Motzen's!!!

Tzipporah and Ephraim Rose

I appreciate Rabbi Yisroel and Rebbetzin Hindy Motzen for their wisdom, kindness and generosity. You make Ner Tamid a home for everyone. We are truly blessed to have you has our leader, teacher and guide.

Irma Pretsfelder

Insightful. Courageous. Authentic. A meturgeman of Torah-true Judaism in the vein of R' Hirsch. Your shul and the entire Baltimore community are blessed to have such a rav.

Robert Rubovitz

We learn that one who teaches Torah to another is like their parent. Not only have I benefited spiritually from the teaching of the Rabbi and Rebbetzin, but I have also had the incredible zechus to find a bonus family at Ner Tamid. Thank you for being the catalysts for the kind of growth, development, connection, and joy I had never dreamed of. Mazel tov!

Sara Rubovitz

Mazel Tov on this well-deserved honor!

The Schuchmans

Rabbi Yisrael and Rebbetzin Hindy Motzen:

Thank you for your leadership, guidance, compassion, and dedication to Ner Tamid over these last 10+ years. You are both a true Kiddush Hashem, and your tremendous efforts over these past 10+ years have not only greatly benefitted our shul and its growth, but also our community, and Klal Yisrael as a whole.

With Great Honor and Respect.
Chanie and Paul Schuster

We are so grateful to be able to learn from you each Shabbat and Yom Tov. May the words in this publication allow this inspiration to be shared with many others. Thank you for educating and guiding us with your thoughts and insights.

Max and Sara Shapiro and Family

Rabbi and Hindy Motzen,

Mazel Tov on your first
ten years with Ner Tamid.
Thanks for all you have
accomplished. Looking
forward to your next ten
years and all you will
get done.

*Harriet Shiffman
Sorah Korenberg
Nancy, Frankie, Ella and
Tyler Lipira*

Mazel Tov to Rabbi and
Rebbetzin Motzen.

*Roberta and
Scott Steppa*

Dear Rabbi Sruli and
Rebbetzin Hindy,

With love and respect we wish
you congratulations on your
prestigious achievements.
Your honesty, integrity, love,
faith, loyalty and character
are the foundation stones of
your success. You have made
us so proud. We daven that
you achieve much happiness
and success in the future
and continue to grow in
your accomplishments.

Love, Safta and Zadie Shur

Thank you to Rabbi
and Rebbetzin Motzen
for all that you do.
Through your wisdom
and chen you are able
to reach everyone,
where they are, with
inspiration and growth.

Jennifer and Neil Stiber

Mazel Tov to Rabbi and Rebbetzin Motzen on this well-deserved honor. With gratitude for your wonderful leadership.

Phyllis and Daniel Sykes

Thank you to Rabbi and Rebbetzin Motzen for all you do each and every day in developing a shul that is not just a shul, but a community in and of itself.

*Shimon and
Chaya Weichbrod*

Thank you To Rabbi Yisrael and Hindy Motzen for bringing warmth, spirit and meaningful learning to Ner Tamid and the community at large.

Sonny Taragin

Dear Motzen Family,

Congratulations to you all on 10 years of amazing service to this community. You have gone above and beyond to extend yourselves to your congregants and myself and for that I am truly grateful. It's wonderful to see your smiling faces and your visits are heartwarming and mean the world to me. Hatzlacha, good mazel and much bracha to each of you for the many years ahead.

Sondra Willner

Wishing mazal tov to
Rabbi and Rebbetzin
Motzen on 10 years of
outstanding service to
the community. May
you continue to make
a difference in the lives
of so many.

Yossi and Esti Ziffer

Li'iluy nishmas Dov Ber Ben Chaim and Chava bas Shlomo Yeshaya
Heneson, former members of Ner Tamid.

Miriam Adler

Thank you to Rabbi Motzen who goes out his way
to visit, and his kind and uplifting manner.

Sybil Wach Barer

Mazal Tov, Rabbi and Rebbetzin Motzen, on the past 10
years! Looking forward to being a part of the next ten!

Yael and Michael Bates

Thank you, Rabbi Yisrael and Rebbetzin Hindy
Motzen, for everything you do for Ner Tamid!

Yehuda & Leah Baumer

Mazel Tov and Kol HaKavod to the wonderful Motzens.
With much HaKoras HaTov for all of the Chesed and
amazing things you do and accomplish.

Sharon Bennett

With tremendous appreciation for these years of phenomenal
leadership by our Rabbi and Rebbetzin! Yasher koach!!

Marc Berman and Abby Sattell

Mazel Tov!!

Nancy Berman

In honor of Rabbi and Hindy Motzen for all that they do for our family, our Kehilla, the entire community, and Klal Yisroel!

Shlomo and Adina Berman

In honor of Rabbi & Mrs. Motzen and all they do for the community and in honor of the most amazing Adina.

Yeshaya and Shoshana Berzon

Mazel tov Rabbi and Rebbetzin Moten on your ten-year anniversary!

Sharie Blum

Mazal tov!! Keep up the great work!

Anonymous

In Honor of Rabbi and Rebbetzin Motzen.

Joe and Helaine Bondar

Mazel Tov Rabbi and Rebbetzin Motzen on 10 years of leadership, guidance and support of the Baltimore community and beyond! Looking forward to celebrating many more years together with you both.

Tamara and Moe Breitowitz

Thank you for helping us grow!

Miryam Canas Silberfarb

It's a pleasure to donate in honor of the area's finest speaker!

Anonymous

In honor of Rabbi Yisrael and Rebbetzin Motzen and the 10 years so far!

Barbara Carter

Baltimore and Ner Tamid are so fortunate to have you both. Thank you for dedicating your life to the klal and for the ongoing support you have provided us.

Tsiona and Yaakov Cohen

Thank you, Rabbi and Rebbetzin Motzen, for the very warm welcome to the shul. Nati and I look forward every week to be with the Ner Tamid community.

Toby Coleman

May you continue to build a beautiful community.

Caren Cutler

Our gratitude for all you have given to our community, Rabbi Motzen.

Marjorie Edelman

With appreciation for the COVID davening tent when we needed it.

Daniel Edelman

Ad Maeh VeEsrim+ to the Rav and Rebbetzin and our very own Adina B.

Family N Edinger, Baltimore/Atlanta

With profound gratitude to Rabbi and Rebbetzin Motzen for their tireless efforts on behalf of Ner Tamid and all its congregants, and in celebration of the Ner Tamid synagogue and community.

David and Ruthie Eisenberg

B'H for 10 times 10 more years. Thank you Rabbi
Yisrael and Rebbetzin Hindy Motzen for the mitzvot you do for
the Ner Tamid Congregation and the Baltimore community.

Abraham & Liliane Elgamil

Thank you for teaching me Succah all those years
ago and continuing to teach me today!

Eli and Ahuva Englander

With tremendous gratitude to Rabbi and Rebbetzin Motzen. May you
continue to be matzliach in your holy mission to support klal yisroel.

Hadassah Eventsur

In honor of the Motzens. Your leadership is inspiring.

Mark and Elana Feld

Thank you, Rabbi and Rebbetzin Motzen, for your
important leadership in the Shul and the community.

Nisa and Ryan Felps

Thank you for everything. You are both amazing people.
You have helped us grow and continue to help us. You
both make us want to be a better people.

Helayne and Scott Ference

In honor Rabbi Motzen and the tireless work he does to better Klal
Yisrael, starting in Baltimore and emanating beyond. May he and
his Rebbetzin have continued strength and siyata dishmaya.

Alexandra and Daniel Fleksher

In honor of the formidable Rabbi and Rebbetzin Motzen!
May you continue to shine your special light!

Atara and Dov Frankel

Thank you Rabbi and Rebbetzin! Your devotion,
enthusiasm, and spirituality are contagious!

Binyamin and Esther Friedman

In memory of Yisroel Yehuda Ben HaRav Chaim Rephael

Joshua Friedman

Thank you both for all you do for the community!

Tamar Frydman

Thank you for being a light that ignites so many souls.

Avraham and Madalyn Frydman

Thank you for your warmth, wisdom, kindness and leadership.

Shana and Marc Frydman-Wilkenfeld

Wonderful community and leaders. Thank you.

Faye G

We have enjoyed our times visiting your synagogue
& look forward to our next visit.

Collen Geisen

Rabbi & Rebbetzin,

Thank you for everything that you do for our entire community.

מחיל אל חיל.

Arie and Dina Glazer

In honor of Rabbi and Mrs. Motzen

Lisa Glick

To Rabbi Yisrael and Rebbetzin Hindy Motzen,

ברכך השס מציון וראה בטוב ירושלים.

Thank you,

Orit Gnatt

Tzippi and Doniel Goetz

In honor of Rabbi Yisrael and Rebbetzin Hindy Motzen.
Yasher koach on your great work for our community!

Rabbi Menachem and Bracha Goldberger

In honor of Rabbi & Rebbetzin Motzen.

Stacey Goldenberg

Mazel tov Rabbi and Rebbetzin Motzen. May you
have many more years at Ner Tamid!

Dr. Manny and Noa Goldman

In honor of Rabbi Yisrael and Rebbetzin Hindy Motzen. With
heartfelt thanks for your continued inspiration and warmth.

Roberta Goldman

Wishing mazal tov to the Motzens on this milestone, and thanks for so many years of Torah and community even for those of us who no longer live in Baltimore.

Talia Goldman

In honor of our wonderful friends!

Moshe and Nanci Grossman

In honor of Rabbi Motzen and all that he does for klal Yisroel.

Ari Grubner

Continued Hatzlacha!

Gary Guttenberg

Thank you for keeping the dream alive!

Ann Halpern

With appreciation and great respect for the outstanding dedication and leadership of Rav and Rebbetzin Motzen whose hearts encompass the entire community.

שליבם הוא לב כל קהל ישראל.

Moshe and Mindi Hauer

Dear Rabbi Motzen, thank you for your kindness and inspiration. It is a pleasure to work with you.

Hannah Heller, Elliot Heller, Gila and Rob Golder

Thank you for all which you do for the community!

Adena and Tzvi Hefter

In honor and appreciation of Rabbi & Rebbetzin Motzen.
Rivka Heisler

In honor of Rabbi Motzen and Rebbetzin Motzen.
Michael Hirsh

Mazel tov and thank you, Rabbi Motzen for your
wonderful Thursday morning shiur!
Chaim and Zahava Hochberg

In honor and amazed by the unbelievable
accomplishments of Rabbi Sruli & Hindy Motzen.
Shana Hoffman

Thanks to Rabbi and Rebbetzin Motzen for their leadership.
Dr. Hogans and the Murinson family

Mazel Tov to Rabbi & Hindy Motzen! Thank you for your support,
kindness, caring, words of wisdom and dedication to Ner Tamid and
our family. We wish your family continued health, happiness and
hatzlacha! May we celebrate many more 10-year anniversaries together!
Barbara & Dan Howarth

Rabbi and Rebbetzin Motzen: yelchu m'chayil el chayil!
Yedida Insel-Sloan

Thank you, Rabbi and Rebbetzin Motzen, for all that you do for the Shul!
Yitzchak and Frannie Jakobi

In honor of Rabbi and Rebbetzin Motzen.

Abraham Kaplansky

In honor of the one and only Adina B/Tante Adina, Ahuva, and Tehilla; and with admiration for Rabbi and Rebbetzin Motzen, all that they have accomplished in their first decade at Ner Tamid, and all that they continue to do for our family, their kehilla, and the Baltimore Jewish community!

Jacob and Eli Kates

Uri and Vivi Kesselman

In honor of my chaver, Rav Yisrael. Behatzlacha Rabbah with the tremendous work you are doing.

Dovid Kimche

In honor of Rabbi and Rebbetzin Motzen and the incredible work they do on behalf of the klal!

Leslie and Chaim Klein

Thank you for your hard work and courage in making Baltimore better!

Aviva and Shalom Kovacs

To our wonderful aunt and uncle who have taught us so much about becoming the people others honor us for being.

Malka and Eli Kravitz

Mazel Tov Rabbi & Rebbetzin Motzen on 10 inspiring years! May you both continue to go from strength to strength!

Ben Kristall-Weiss

To the esteemed Rabbi and Rebbetzin for everything
they do for the shul and all of Klal Yisrael.

Judah Labovitz

I wish we lived less than two kilometers away.
Yaacov Meir ben Gedalia HaLevi & Martha (Minda) Landaw
In honor of Rabbi Motzen and his Rebbetzin for all they do!

Naftali and Baila Langer

Mazel Tov on your first 10 years. May you go from Strength to Strength
in the next 10 years. Thank you for your leadership in making Ner
Tamid a welcoming place for all in the Baltimore community.

Elly and Shayndee Lasson

Thanks for all you do for the shul and community.

The Lazerows, Carters, and Mullers

In honor of Rabbi and Rebbetzin Motzen and all they
do for the greater Baltimore community.

Chaya Lencz

In honor of our wonderful friends, Sara and
Max! In memory of Edan Shapiro.

Dena Lerner

Mazal Tov on this milestone! May you be blessed with
continued growth & success and in good health always!

Lisa and Irwin Lotwin

Thank you for all that you do and inspiring us!!

Moshe Marcus

In honor of the wonderful Rabbi and Rebbetzin!

Rabbi Binyamin and Dr. Miriam Marwick

Wishing You Continued Success and Happiness.

Liz and Mitch Mayer

Wishing Rabbi Motzen many more years of success.

Mordy and Lisa Meister

Mazel Tov on your 10-year anniversary!

Mark and Robyn Melzer

There are not enough words or time to express the gratitude I have for both of you and the community you've created! Thank you!!!

Rivkah Esther Merville

Mazal Tov!

Barb and Blaine Mischel

In honor of the Motzens' incredible work and the Polirers' consistent support of the shul's initiatives

Bari Mitzmann

In honor of an amazing couple Sruli and Hindy (we would say that even if we weren't related).

AD and Shifra Motzen

Ya'asher Koach on all the time, work, and energy
you put into creating a beautiful shul!

You should continue to be Matzliach and may
you be showered with brachos!

Sarah Motzen

Hatzlacha and Congratulations to the Motzen Family!

Myrowitz Family

Mazel tov to Rabbi and Rebbetzin Motzen! Till 120 in good health.

Shera Nusbaum

In honor of Rabbi and Rebbetzin Motzen, who lead by
example, with compassion, sensitivity, and courage when
needed. May Hashem reward your holy work tenfold.

Yossi and Yona Openden

Amazing Shul - Amazing Environment - I have seen
the effort of Rabbi and Rebbetzin Motzen growing Ner
Tamid into a very welcoming place for everyone!

Joelah and Israel Orange

In honor of Rabbi & Rebbetzin Motzen, Chava, Morah
Ayala, Morah Stephanie, and Morah Tamara!

Natan and Hayley Orlofsky

Thank you Rabbi & Rebbetzin Motzen for your dedicated
leadership. Looking forward to the next 10 years together!

Zev and Ayala Pensak

With much hakaras hatov to Rabbi and Rebbetzin Motzen.
Shkoyach for all you do to enhance our wonderful community!

Margie Pensak

May this small contribution, sent with lots of love,
support you in reaching your goal.

Edwin Perez

Thank you for all your hard work and all you do for
the Ner Tamid Congregation! Mazal Tov!

Nili Pinchasin

We are happy that you are a part of our family's daily life.
We hope your future is as bright as your smile.

Rena and Sheldon Polun

With tremendous Hakarat Hatov for your dedication to your
admirers from across the ocean. Chizku V'imtzu.

Barbie and Glenn Porcelain

Thank you for all you do for the Ner Tamid and
larger Baltimore community as well!

Liora Quartey

In honor of Rabbi & Rebbetzin Motzen and in
recognition of their leadership & the warm, welcoming
environment they have created at Ner Tamid.

Also, thank you Adina B for all that you do
for this Shul and our community.

Jodi Reches

Mazal Tov!

Thank you Rabbi and Rebbetzin Motzen for all
that you do on behalf of the Community.

Suri & Barry Reiner

Thank you for creating a place where everyone feels at home.

Naami Resnick

Mazel tov on this very special occasion. May Hashem bless
you and your beautiful family with good health, happiness
and the ability to continue doing the amazing work you have
done at Ner Tamid for MANY more years to come.

Mindy Rose/Howard

Thank you for all that you do for the community. Your warmth and
sensitivity are evident with everything you do. Thanks especially
for your continued dedication to the singles in our community!

Rachel Rosenberg

In honor of Rabbi & Rebbetzin Motzen, Hava, Morah
Ayala, Morah Stephanie, and Morah Tamara!

Shalom and Elana Rosenberg

It's challenging to be a rabbi and rebbetzin of a non-homogeneous
shul, but you do it with a commitment to Judaism and a commitment
to kindness. You have set an example of being welcoming and
not exclusive. May you go from strength to strength!

Sarah Rosenbloom

Mazel tov!!

Devorah Rosenbloom

In honor of Rabbi & Mrs. Motzen - Thank you for
all you do for the community and beyond!

Azi and Riki Rosenblum

In honor of Rabbi and Rebbetzin Motzen.

Ellen and Erik Roskes

Mazel tov Rebbetzin Hindy! May you keep growing
to greater heights and taking others with you!

Sara Rachel Salhanick

In honor of the Motzens and their contribution to our
community and in honor of Adina Burstyn for her
dedication to making our city a better place!!!

Andrea and Ari Schulman

Mazel tov to Rabbi and Rebbetzin Motzen on their first 10 years at Ner
Tamid. We are blessed with a pair of rock stars, and I look forward to
helping you both realize your vision for the shul and for Klal Yisrael.

Debbie Schwartz

Thank you for all that you do.

Benzion Shamberg

In appreciation for all that you do and for the example you set.

Marc and Gwen Shar

In honor of Rabbi Motzen.

Margie Shulman

Mazel Tov to Rabbi and Rebbetzin Motzen on this well-deserved honor.

Yakov Shuster

Thank you to Rabbi and Rebbetzin Motzen for everything you
do for the community. We especially appreciate the support
and guidance you have given to our family over the years.
May you continue to go from strength to strength!

Reeut and Nadav Singerman

In honor of Rabbi and Rebbetzin Motzen for
their dedication to the community.

Daniel and Ruchama Skurnik

In honor of adina b. Mazel tov to the Motzens on 10 years!

Bryna Sperling

In honor of Rabbi and Rebbetzin Motzen for their selfless
commitment and service to the community.

Stacy and David Spiegelman

Mazel Tov to Rabbi & Rebbetzin Motzen.

Peter Sterba and Ellen Soltz

In honor of Rabbi and Rebbetzin Motzen. Thank you
for everything you do for the community!

Devorah Stern

To two amazing people and role models! We appreciate everything you do.

Ari and Esti Taragin

Rabbi Motzen and Hindy. Hatzlacha in everything you
do. We are in awe of your leadership at Ner Tamid.

Tova and Alan Taragin

Thank you for always welcoming us to your shul when we visit Baltimore.

Shoshana, David and Tova Teichman

Thank you to Rabbi and Mrs. Motzen for their incredible
leadership and dedication. Mazel tov on 10 years!

Itael Toibman

Thank you for the kindness, empathy, and wisdom you
have shown us in so many ways over the past decade.

Susan Tomchin

In honor of Rabbi Motzen and in appreciation of the
Sunday morning Women's Halacha shiur.

Karyn Toso

Thank you for all you do for the community.

CR and Tzvi Urszuy

Beautiful 10th anniversary celebration. Wishing the Motzen Family
only the best going forward. Good luck and good health.

Charlie Venick

To a most deserving and wonderful Rabbi and Rebbetzin
- Mazal tov on this wonderful milestone!!

Marthe Vidaver

To a most deserving and wonderful Rabbi and Rebbetzin
- Mazal tov on this wonderful milestone!!

Dovid and Elisheva Weinberger

In honor of Rabbi and Rebbetzin Motzen and all they do for Klal Yisrael!

Jason Weinblatt

In support of Rabbi and Rebbetzin Motzen.

Evan and Dina Weiner

In memory of Ilan Ganeles.

Attorney Ruth Weissman

In honor of Rabbi and Rebbetzin Motzen.

Ben and Lana Wise

In honor of Hindy's first sermon.

Nechama and Binyamin Wisotsky

Thank you, Rabbi Motzen, for being a voice and support to all
members of our community. I am honored to be a part of your
community and call you my Rav. Thank you for the thought-
provoking conversations and never judging. Thank you for your
guidance and unwavering support and for A Single Impact and
making Ner Tamid a welcoming atmosphere for all. Thank you.

Rochel Ziman

To two deserving people who I am proud to know, Rabbi Yisroel Motzen and his hard-working and creative partner, Hindy. I have watched this synagogue grow so spiritually and am very proud of you both. May you continue to have the health and energy to give such careful thought to each of your takes on the weekly portion. I, for one, enjoy and learn from them. Upwards and onwards, my wonderful grandson. Love, Bubby.

With Love, Bubby Marion Zweiter